START RIGHT

Success Habits for International Students

BORIS REMES

START RIGHT
Success Habits for International Students

Copyright © 2020. Boris Remes.
Published by iStartRight Books, a division of Remes Inc.

StartRightBook.com

All rights reserved. No part of this publication may be reproduced, distributed, or transmitted in any form or by any means, including photocopying, recording, or other electronic or mechanical methods, without the prior written permission of the publisher, except in the case of brief quotations embodied in critical reviews and certain other non-commercial uses permitted by copyright law.

Print ISBN: 978-1-7770900-1-2
Digital ISBN: 978-1-7770900-0-5

Copy editing by Peggy Herring
Cover photograph by Gordon Hawkins
Layout by www.formatting4U.com

Remes Inc.
6D - 7398 Yonge St, Unit # 627
Thornhill, ON L4J 8J2
Canada

Disclaimer: The author makes no guarantees concerning the level of success you may experience following the advice and strategies in this book, and you accept that results will differ for each individual. The examples provided show exceptional results, which may not apply to the average reader, and are not intended to imply that you will achieve the same or similar outcomes.

Dedication

To the current, future, and past international students for inspiring me to write this book.

Even if just one idea here helps you, I will be utterly grateful and fulfilled.

Table of Contents

About the Author i

Introduction iii

What Will This Book Do for You? vii

Chapter 1: Why Studying Abroad is Important 1
   The Paradigm Shift 2
   Personal Growth 4
   How Else Will You Be Able to Benefit? 6
   Make Sure You Are Prepared (It's Not for
   Everyone) 6
   Exercise: Try It Out 7

Chapter 2: Why Study in Canada? 9
   Quality of Life 10
   Multiculturalism and Diversity 11
   Nature 12
   A World-Class Education System 12
   Your Career 13
   Proximity to the U.S. 14
   Exercise: Research Where You Want to Go 15

Chapter 3: Success Habits to Start Right 17
   Become Disciplined 17
   Develop Language Skills 18
   Set Goals 20
   "But, Boris, I Don't Know What I Want!" 24
   Exercise: Start Setting Goals Now 25

Chapter 4: How and Where to Get Answers to Your Questions 27
   Do Your Research 28
   Reach Out to People to Get More Information 29
   Exercise: Start a List of Potential Contacts 34

Chapter 5: How to Choose a School/Program 35
   Listen to Your Heart and Your Intuition 36
   How to Read Rankings 37
   Location, Location, Location! 38
   Assess Fit 38
   Don't Take Anything at Face Value 39
   Take Your Time to Ensure You Make the Right Decision 40
   Exercise: Time to Start Your School Decision Matrix 41

Chapter 6: How to Fund Your Studies 43
   Savings 43
   Scholarships 44
   Employment During Studies 45
   Loan Programs 46
   Exercise: Create a Budget 46

Chapter 7: Applying to Your School 49
   How to Apply 49
   What You Need to Apply 50
   How Your Application is Evaluated 51
   Choose the Best Offer 52
   Apply for a Visa 53
   Exercise: Prepare Your Documentation 53

Chapter 8: Arriving in Canada 55
   Pack 56
   Double Check Your Documentation 57
   Exercise: Find and Face Your Fear 58

Chapter 9: The First 90 Days.. 59
  What Habits Do You Need to Succeed in the First 90
  Days?.. 60
  Put First Things First 61
  Deal with Culture Shock... 64
  Avoid the Cultural Bubble.. 66
  Learn the Cultural Norms 66
  Learn English Fast 67
  Make Canadian Friends 69
  Exercise: Break the Ice with Conversation Starters 75
  Get a Buddy 76
  Manage Relationships Back Home............................ 76
  Manage Stress 77
  What to Do If You Get Sick 80
  Exercise: Get Fit 81
  Be Proactive... 82
  Begin with the End in Mind....................................... 82
  Get to Know the Teachers/Professors........................ 83
  Get a Mentor 84
  Model Behaviour 85
  Don't Take Bad Advice 86
  Get Good Grades 87
  Exercise: What's Cool About You?........................... 93

Chapter 10: The First Year in Canada.......................... 95
  What Habits Do You Need to Succeed in the First
  Year?... 95
  Be Solution Oriented 96
  Exercise: Stay Happy... 97
  Improve Your Leadership Skills................................ 98
  Say Yes, Figure Out the Rest, and Don't Take No
  for an Answer... 99
  Exercise: Do Anywhere Gratitude........................... 100
  Manage Your Finances 101

   Build Your Personal Brand 102
   Exercise: Personal Brand for Career Success 106

Chapter 11: Transitioning to the Job Market 109
   Keep Building Your Network 109
   Get a Part-Time Job 111
   Get a Summer Internship 115
   Interview for a Job 115
   Negotiate Your Salary 118
   File Taxes 122
   Get Micro-Credentials 123
   What's the Difference Between a Job, a Career, and a Life Mission? 123
   Exercise: Personal Reflection and Introspection Essay 124

Chapter 12: Transitioning to Permanent Residency 127
   Who is Eligible? 127
   Exercise: Study for Citizenship 128

Chapter 13: Success Habits for a Lifetime 131
   Exercise: Stay in Balance 131
   Exercise: Gain Clarity 132

Conclusion 135

A Note to Parents 137

About the Author

Boris Remes is an award-winning education marketer, entrepreneur, speaker, and author. Boris left Almaty, Kazakhstan as an international student at the age of sixteen. He lived and worked in Vancouver and Toronto in Canada, studied on exchange in Paris, France, and has visited more than sixty countries in the past six years.

Boris started his career in marketing, recruitment, admissions, and program development for Bodwell High School, an international boarding school in North Vancouver, Canada. In his role, Boris supported more than 1,000 international students and their families. In 2015, Boris received the *Excellence in International Education Marketing Award* from the British Columbia Council for International Education.

He then moved across the country to lead specialized graduate management and executive programs at the Schulich School of Business, York University in Toronto. In this role, Boris worked with more than 400 international professionals in their pursuit of master's degrees and executive programs.

As a Manager of Higher Education Consulting at Deloitte, Boris delivered strategy and technology consulting projects for universities, colleges, and public sector clients, both in Canada and internationally.

Boris holds a Bachelor of Commerce with honours from the University of British Columbia, and a Master of Business Administration with distinction from the Schulich School of Business, York University.

He enjoys competing in triathlons, geeking out about travel miles and points, taking his family on adventure trips, and attending spiritual and meditation retreats.

Boris enjoys reading business and personal growth books. To see his reading list, go to **StartRightBook.com/resources.**

His motto is, "To whom much is given, much will be expected."

Introduction

Have you been thinking about studying in Canada as an international student?

Are you stressed out about it?

Are you worried about making friends, living away from your family, and managing finances?

Or, are you further ahead in your studies, and now wanting to find the best way to land a dream job after graduation?

Well, I faced exactly the same questions myself when I was an international student. Over 15 years ago, I bought a one-way ticket, left my family in Kazakhstan, and came to Canada, a country where I did not know a single person. I had to figure out everything myself through trial and error. I often wished there had been a guidebook to help me start right—a book written by someone who had already blazed this trail.

Today, I know something about the answers to those questions. Because over the years, I have helped thousands of students enrolled in everything from summer courses to high school to bachelor and graduate level programs to plan, apply, arrive, and successfully settle in Canada. I have also helped many of those students prepare for and enter the job market. And it's not just students. Many of their parents were also able to benefit from my education, experience, and training.

My first "client" was my brother David. My parents sent him to join me in Canada just before I graduated from university. I coached him in the lessons I'd learned in the preceding years, and he followed in my footsteps. My parents fairly compensated me for my services, and, to everyone's surprise, I turned that experience into a full-time career in international education.

In this book, I want to share secrets to success which will help you to apply for and get into education programs in Canada, navigate cultural, academic, and professional settings, and, most importantly, grow intellectually, physically, emotionally, spiritually, and professionally.

My system and advice are proven to work, and I want many more prospective and current students to START RIGHT and continue their journeys in Canada. I dreamed of having a better life abroad, and I worked hard and smart to get where I am right now. I went from being a foreigner to being a proud Canadian citizen, and I want you to also achieve whatever dreams you have. It will take time and effort, but, with the help of this book, I believe you can do it.

Let me tell you about an educational challenge I faced. When I was growing up, my parents put a lot of pressure on me to read. I was impatient, and I found the books they gave me impractical. I appreciate Russian literature, but it was difficult to relate to characters living in Tsarist Russia or the collapsing Soviet Union. I would do everything possible to get out of reading 60 minutes per day—which was the length of time then prescribed under the Soviet curriculum. I also later discovered that my reading and writing skills were inferior to my classmates', which affected my confidence. I would be embarrassed to read in front of them. Sometimes they would laugh and, once, my elementary school teacher secretly removed me from the classroom because the government school inspector was scheduled to appear.

To make things worse, I was diagnosed with minor dyslexia, which certainly did not help matters. However, instead of letting fear hold me back, I learned to face it. I developed public speaking skills with the help of a teacher who guided me toward public speaking opportunities. This led to further opportunities. I won a prize in a Kazakh poetry competition, even though I do not speak Kazakh.

I still tend to be a slow reader and a poor writer. I'm not the kind of person you'd expect would write a book. But I decided to challenge myself. As I have before, I took my fears about reading and writing, faced them, and found that eventually I was able to toss them aside. This book exists only because, with the right help and support, I was able to face my fears and transform them into action.

You can do the same. People conquer their fears when they put their minds to it. Studying in Canada showed me that. It has been one of the best things I've done in my life, and I truly believe it could be right for you, as well.

In this book, you will find advice and tips, along with some resources that will be very useful throughout the entire cycle of your studies, from leaving your home culture to eventually becoming a global citizen.

This book comes with a workbook, a list of my favourite personal growth and business books, and other bonuses which can be accessed by going to **StartRightBook.com/resources**.

What Will This Book Do for You?

Did you know that international students (and their parents) contribute billions of dollars to the Canadian economy? Did you know that these students are an essential source of skilled workers and that many will become immigrants to the country? It's true! You are a BIG deal!

Having said that, if you choose this path, you will be expected to figure out a lot, on your own, in a brief period of time. There is a lot of pressure and expectation to navigate through academic, cultural, and professional adaptation, and develop self-advocacy.

But help is available. Over the years, I have developed a holistic system which allows international students to be successful with planning, applying, and arriving to study, work, and live in Canada. I want to share this wisdom, and the harmony it's brought me. I want international students to realize their full potential and become contributing members of Canadian society.

The advice, personal stories, practical tips, and exercises in this book can help you succeed. My goal is to provide you, or, if you're a parent, your daughter or son, with a compact and cohesive guide that will help ensure success.

Every chapter of this book mentions certain habits that have brought me and other international students success in studying, working, and living in a new country. If you can develop habits that make you self-accepting, confident, and courageous, you're more likely to reach your full potential.

What is a habit? The way I look at it, a habit is something that's part of your character, and it becomes so automatic that you don't need to think about it. Success habits make you productive. They're a kind of superpower. If you're open to new ideas and coachable, you will be able to adopt the success habits which will take you to the next level in life.

You are just one habit away from getting into your dream school. You are just one habit away from getting an "A." You are just one habit away from graduation. You are just one habit away from your dream job. You are just one habit away from your dream life.

Depending on where you are in your journey, you can start from the beginning of this book, or just dive into the chapter that seems most relevant to where you are today.

In Chapters 1 and 2, you will learn about the benefits of studying abroad, and in Canada, in particular. In Chapter 3, I will tell you about the habits that are needed to START RIGHT. Chapter 4 reveals where and how to get information on schooling, while Chapter 5 covers how to choose a school and a program. Chapter 6 delves into funding your studies. In Chapter 7, you will find out how to apply for school, and in Chapter 8, you will learn what to do to get ready to head to Canada. Chapter 9 goes over the important things to do during your first 90 days, and Chapter 10 covers your first year in Canada. Chapter 11 goes beyond school and talks about transitioning to the job market, and in Chapter 12, I talk about getting permanent residency and Canadian citizenship. Chapter 13 is about the success habits that will serve you for the rest of your life. Finally, there's a special note for parents.

There's a lot to learn, so let's get started.

Chapter 1: Why Studying Abroad is Important

"Education is the passport to the future, for tomorrow belongs to those who prepare for it today." – Malcolm X

The idea of studying abroad can be very alluring. It sounds fun and exciting, and it certainly can be. It can also be one of the biggest and best opportunities of your life. It can and will change you for the better when you do it RIGHT. Studying abroad can take you places and show you things you never dreamed were possible. However, I want this book to be honest and helpful. So, you should know that despite the many rewards waiting for you on the other side, travelling to a new land can be intimidating and frightening.

Whether you are just now heading out on your own, or you have been by yourself overseas for a few years, experiences like these sometimes feel overwhelming. You certainly do not want to let your parents down, and you do not want to have to come back home. The last thing you want is to waste money and feel like a failure. It's natural. I felt the same way. Everyone gets scared doing something like this, even if they put on a brave face to hide it. I certainly did. Understand that it is *okay* to be frightened. But you will need to conquer this fear, and one of the best ways to truly get a hold of your anxiety and harness it is to make a plan.

I was a rebellious teenager. I challenged my teachers and even the principal back in Kazakhstan on their teaching methods and values. Once, I organized a walk-out of students because the principal fired my favourite geography teacher without cause—at least that was how I saw it. I was a very capable kid, but I could not stay focused. My parents wanted a better future for me and realized that my potential would not be fully realized in the environment I was in. So, they created a plan for me to execute.

In this chapter, we will look at several reasons to consider studying abroad and analyze just why it might be important for you.

The Paradigm Shift

One of the first things you need to realize when it comes to studying abroad is that it will be a paradigm shift. It will require that you change your view on how things work and what you should expect. After all, you will be stepping outside of the comfortable cultural realm in which you were raised.

Simply put, it means you will be changing the way you think and do things. This doesn't mean you will leave your culture behind or that you will forget where you're from or who you are. It just means you will be expanding your horizons and possibilities, which is an enriching experience. For me, visiting new places, meeting new people, and enjoying new foods nourished my mind, which completely transformed my perspective on this world.

What I have discovered is that the only way to see what is inside yourself is by jumping out of your comfort zone or, as it was in my case, having your parents throw you into a completely new environment. Sure, it can be nerve-wracking to have to face challenging situations, but it helps you become more mature and self-confident.

I remember coming home during the summer break, after finishing Grade 11 in Vancouver, and meeting my friends. We were still close, but I was not the same. Though we shared many common interests, my horizons had expanded, and I saw the world in different colours. I had gained a completely different appreciation of the freedom I was seeking as a teenager.

When you are an international student, you will meet a wide variety of interesting people. You may make friends with people from different cultures and backgrounds, which gives you a different point of view of the world. Moreover, when you are finally able to adapt and get past that initial culture shock, you will not be as reluctant to move abroad in the future. It's a positive experience and many well-established companies appreciate when employees have already developed this skill.

Immersing yourself in a different country provides you with an opportunity to learn or master the country's language at social, academic, and professional levels. You will also gain expertise in interpersonal communications and become emotionally intelligent.

If you want to foster success while experiencing such a paradigm shift, you should develop habits such as adaptability and mobility. See change as a positive that will expand your horizons. Such habits are huge assets in the modern world and can help take you to places you have never dreamed of before.

Personal Growth

The paradigm shift and the change in your environment can help you improve as a person. After all, you are not going to a new land and getting an education just so you can stagnate and remain who you always were. It will be a time of personal growth, and you might as well embrace it.

Studying abroad is a time of immense personal growth. You will not only be learning new things in the courses you take, but you will also be learning about a brand-new culture. Take it in and experience the change. Globalize yourself. Learn the ways of the new culture and adapt. It can take some time, but if you prepare yourself even before you leave home, it will help.

The more you can learn about the culture and what to expect from the place where you will be studying, working, and living, the better off you will be. As you learn the new norms, you will begin to feel more at home in the new environment.

Studying abroad is one of the most powerful experiences you will ever have. I cannot imagine who I would be today without the transformative power of my international education. It is through this experience that I realized the only thing holding me back is ME, and that the only way I can experience change is if I take action.

You can't expect others to change *your* life for you. After all, change begins with you.

Take this story, which is said to be written on an Anglican bishop's tomb in the crypts of Westminster Abbey in London, England:

> When I was young and free and my imagination had no limits, I dreamed of changing the world. As I grew older and wiser, I discovered the world would not change, so I shortened my sights somewhat and decided to change only my country.
>
> But, it too, seemed immovable.
>
> As I grew into my twilight years, in one last desperate attempt, I settled for changing only my family, those closest to me, but alas, they would have none of it.
>
> And now as I lie on my deathbed, I suddenly realize: If I had only changed myself first, then by

example I would have changed my family. From their inspiration and encouragement, I would then have been able to better my country and, who knows, I may have even changed the world.

How Else Will You Be Able to Benefit?

When you are studying in a different country, the knowledge and skills you gain will help not only in your personal life but in everything that you do going forward. You will develop new life skills that will serve you well. You will meet other students, make new friends, connect with faculty, employers, citizens, and others in the new country. With each experience you have, you will be growing as a person.

With each person you meet, you will develop contacts that have the potential to help you throughout your life. You will be able to advance your interpersonal skills, work skills, and much more, which will, in turn, help advance your career after you have completed your studies.

There are countless benefits to studying abroad. Even though it might be frightening to consider at first, just imagine the adventures and the possibilities that await you.

Make Sure You Are Prepared (It's Not for Everyone)

As great as studying abroad might be, it is not the right option for everyone. Before you decide where you want to go and start applying to schools in that country, you need to be sure you are ready and prepared. Maybe you will want another year or so in your own country to make sure that everything is set, and that you are emotionally ready.

Perhaps, in that process, you will come to the realization that you can't bear to be away from your home and family for that long. Perhaps your finances won't allow you to make the transition to study and live abroad just yet.

If you feel that it is not the right option, don't do it. Moving outside your comfort zone is useful and beneficial, but it's not always the right solution for everyone. Make sure it *is* for you and that you are ready, so you don't get in over your head.

Exercise: Try It Out

If you are still concerned about studying abroad for the long-term, you might want to instead take a short-term language or summer program. This would allow you to test the waters to see how you feel about being away from home.

This is something I did. I studied on exchange in the United Kingdom, as well as in France. These were very important investments my parents made to prepare me for my move to Canada. I gained a better understanding of the local culture and I learned to speak the language. Even though you might be practicing English in your own country, there is nothing that beats immersion in a new country if you want to learn quickly. The experience allows you to know more than just vocabulary and grammar. You start to learn *how* people interact with one another.

Learning the language and improving your accent are essential if you hope to fit in when you arrive. While it might not seem fair that people judge you based on your accent, it happens all the time. We can't change the way people think, but we can improve our language abilities and our presentation.

Chapter 2: Why Study in Canada?

"Living in a foreign country is one of those things that everyone should try at least once…it completed a person, sanding down the rough provincial edges and transforming you into a citizen of the world."– David Sedaris

There are many places around the world that you might be considering for your overseas schooling. The United States, the UK, Australia, and France are all popular choices. However, I believe the best place to get your education is in Canada. The country has a lot to offer. In this chapter, I want to dive deeper and look into some of the best reasons to make Canada your top choice.

For my parents, it was as nerve-wracking as it was for me, of course. No one in my family knew anyone in Canada. However, we still believed it was the right place to go to study, work, and grow as a global citizen. So, off I went with a one-way ticket.

On the outside, I desired independence and freedom like any teenager. I wanted to be successful and make money to get the things I wanted. But, on the inside, I was also afraid of disappointing my parents. I wanted to prove that I was not worthless and that I deserved their love. I also felt responsible, as the eldest, to lead the way for my brothers.

Despite all these voices in my head and emotions in my heart, I was excited, and I tried to keep a positive attitude. I believed that Canada was a better place for me, and I still accept that as true.

Quality of Life

The quality of life in Canada is much higher than in many countries around the world. Technology is widely available, and there is high-quality infrastructure throughout the larger metropolitan areas. The cost of living is reasonable in most locations compared to other developed countries. You will find that it is a welcoming and interesting place to live that you will surely want to call home one day. It's also a safe country compared to so many other locations. Canada ranks first in the world for quality of life in the latest 2019 Best Countries Rankings by U.S. News and World Report. Three Canadian cities—Toronto, Vancouver, and Calgary—are consistently ranked among North America's most livable cities according to the Economist Intelligence Unit.

Let's not forget all the cultural experiences that one can have in Canada. There are museums, art galleries, and various festivals in every province. You will also find that cities have a range of different neighbourhoods, with their own unique flavour and feel. For example, walking down Bloor Street in Toronto, you can enjoy Italian home-style lasagna and authentic gelato, Indian butter chicken and naan, Ukrainian perogies, Portuguese tarts, all on the same street, often even within the same block.

Multiculturalism and Diversity

Canada is a cultural mosaic with a mix of ethnic groups, languages, and cultures that coexist within society. There are two official languages, English and French, but many others are widely spoken within large metropolitan areas such as Toronto, Montreal, and Vancouver.

Canada is a welcoming environment that allows people to retain their customs and traditions. Residents benefit from this diversity. You will find yourself learning about the culture of Canada, but also about the cultures of students who come from countries other than your own. This enriched environment can help expand your horizons and your knowledge of the world and the people surrounding you.

You are essentially entering a brand-new world when you go to school in Canada. Things will be different from where you grew up. The people will be different. However, this isn't a time to shy away and hold onto your past. Diversity is part of a future that you will want to fully embrace.

There is a poem by James Patrick Kinney called "The Cold Within" which reminds me of the danger of the prejudices that exist in people. In the poem, people are trapped in the cold around a dying fire. Each one has a stick to add to the fire, but because of their beliefs about race or social status, they refuse. They eventually die from their arrogance and the cold within their hearts.

The poem shows why diversity is so important. A society made up of different cultures and types of people is stronger. It is important for students to understand this and learn to embrace diversity. Go to **StartRightBook.com/resources** to see a recording of me reading this poem.

Nature

It's hard to talk about Canada without mentioning the natural beauty this country has to offer. If you love the great outdoors, or you would like to experience nature in its pristine form, Canada is a great place for it. You can spend time enjoying the coast on the eastern or western side of the country, or, for the most adventurous, the northern side. You can visit the Rocky Mountains in western Canada, visit the Great Lakes, and find places to hike, fish, swim, ski, mountain bike, canoe, take in the wildlife, and so much more. There are many wonderful things you can do in the great outdoors.

A World-Class Education System

The universities and colleges in Canada are renowned for being some of the best in the world. This is particularly true when it comes to research and innovation. There are many different types of programs that can suit a wide range of career options. A diploma or degree from Canada is seen as equivalent to one earned in the United States, the United Kingdom, or other countries with reputable education systems.

You will also find great value in the education system in Canada. Not only is schooling high-quality, but the cost of tuition tends to be lower than it is in the United Kingdom and the United States. It is competitive when compared to other countries' international tuition fees, as well as in terms of living expenses.

I am fortunate to have graduated from two of the best business schools in the country, and possibly in the world: Sauder School of Business at The University of British Columbia in Vancouver, and the Schulich School of Business at York University in Toronto. To pay my way, I financed my studies through scholarships, personal and family savings, and employment during my studies. I will elaborate on these strategies later in this book. These are truly world-class institutions with innovative programming, global reach, and diverse perspectives.

Your Career

Canada is a country with opportunities around every corner. Those who study and work hard (and occasionally party hard) will find that many career prospects await them. It is often possible to work while you are going to school, depending on the conditions of your study permit. There will be more about study permits later in the book.

The usual path for a student to become a permanent resident in Canada is through a post-graduate work permit. This work permit can be issued after completing a study program for the duration of that program, up to three years. For example, someone who graduated from a four-year program would be eligible for a three-year post-graduate work permit. This can help lead to permanent residency in Canada. However, visa and immigration rules constantly change, so make sure to consult the government website for up to date information.

By meeting students and professors throughout your schooling, as well as others that you encounter during your time in Canada, you can start to make connections. These connections will become part of your network and could help you later with your career, as well as with other aspects of your life.

Lack of local networks is probably one of the weakest links that international students face when pursuing career opportunities in Canada. With such a disadvantage, it is critical to start building networks even when you are in the early stages of your international education journey. LinkedIn is the best platform to start finding and maintaining these connections.

Proximity to the U.S.

Of course, there is also the proximity to the United States. You can be just a short drive or flight from the

United States, which you may want to visit so you can experience the attractions the country offers. Maybe you want to head to Disneyland or Disneyworld. Perhaps you would like to take a trip to New York City or Hollywood. Being next to the United States is undoubtedly a benefit, although you will find so much to enjoy in Canada that you may never head south of the border.

Proximity offers tremendous economic opportunities, since Canada and the U.S. are important trading partners. Many jobs are created and supported through this close relationship. In fact, the U.S. is one of the top ten sources of international students to Canada, and many American students come to Canada for the same reasons as you.

Exercise: Research Where You Want to Go

Many places in Canada have schools that represent all program and budget levels. Once you have decided on a few of the areas that interest you, start doing some in-depth research. Just remember not to overthink. As you study the information, listen to your heart and let your intuition guide you.

For this exercise, you will want to start looking at Canada as a whole, and then, narrow your focus to the academic institutions, programs and locations where you want to study. Learn a bit about the history, culture, and geography. Dive into finding out as much as you can about those schools, locations, neighbourhoods in the city, places to live if you are not going to be in residence, etc. Think about where you might want to dine or areas where you might want to shop. The more you start to learn about the school and the city, the less frightening and more exciting it will be. Think about your favourite musicians and how you might be able to see them play live. Think about your favourite actors. Many Hollywood movies are shot in Canada, and you might just see one of those actors on set in the city you live in. I have seen my fair share of celebrities on the streets of Vancouver. You never know who you will meet on your way to school.

This is a fun exercise that will show you the possibilities and help get your head in the right space to move forward.

Chapter 3: Success Habits to Start Right

"Success is the product of daily habits—not once-in-a-lifetime transformations." – James Clear

You want to make yourself and your parents proud when you study abroad, but success does not happen by accident. It takes careful thought and planning to create a path that will take you where you need to go. Get everything in order before you actually start applying to schools.

Become Disciplined

Discipline is a decision to do something that you don't really like doing in order to achieve something you really want. If you want to succeed, you need to be disciplined. This is just as true in the planning and research stage, as it is when you are at school in Canada. When you are on your own, you won't have your parents around to pick up the slack. They won't be there to remind you to do your schoolwork and make it to class. They won't be there to take care of your laundry, preparing meals, and so many of the other things you might be taking for granted right now.

When you are in another country, if you aren't disciplined enough to take care of yourself, you are not going to have a good time. You might be headed back to your parents sooner than you think. That's the last thing you want!

So, start taking more responsibility right now and become more disciplined. This will be helpful when you are in school, but it will continue to help you for the rest of your personal and professional life.

When I procrastinate and neglect small things such as reading, writing, doing housework, exercising, and meditating, or, much bigger things such as building and maintaining relationships with my family and friends, or advancing my career and life mission, things pile up, and I lose momentum. Only through small, disciplined steps, taken every day, am I able to move the needle on what I really want to achieve in life.

Develop Language Skills

It can't be overstated enough: you will need to develop your language skills. You want to learn the English language, so you don't encounter stumbling blocks when you arrive in Canada. If English is not your first language, take some classes. There are many options online or in-person, in group settings or one-on-one. Change your phone and computer to English, watch American and Canadian movies with subtitles, read books, and listen to podcasts to accelerate your language development.

Go to **StartRightBook.com/resources** to see the programs and tools I recommend to advance your language development.

Let me tell you about a time when my English language skills affected me on a personal level. In Kazakhstan, my father runs a fitness centre with a pool. I was curious about the various health and wellness technologies available in Canada as compared to my home country. So, not too long after I had arrived, I went to a sports equipment store to learn about the cost of a jacuzzi, thinking that perhaps, if the cost wasn't ridiculous, it could be sent to Kazakhstan. I went to the store while wearing my school uniform, and, in my broken English, I asked the manager about the price of hot tubs. He gave me a strange look, and then said he did not want to talk to me. I asked him why, and he told me to leave. I found out later the reason the manager would not speak to me was because he knew I was an international student, and he believed that my parents were in the mafia. I was devastated. It was shocking and painful to be misjudged, and I really did not know how to handle it. I felt very upset, as you can imagine.

It became essential for me to improve my English and my presentation skills, so I could avoid situations like that and become instead an excellent ambassador for international students. Spend some time improving your English skills. Taking a short language program before committing to an academic program can be the perfect solution.

Set Goals

A quote from *Alice in Wonderland* provides some insight into why it's important to have goals.

> "Would you tell me, please, which way I ought to go from here?"
> "That depends a good deal on where you want to get to," said the Cat.
> "I don't much care where–" said Alice.
> "Then it doesn't matter which way you go," said the Cat.

Without goals, how do you measure how well or how poorly you are doing? How do you determine whether you are still on the right path, or if you need to reroute and get your focus back? Learning how to set goals properly will set you up for success.

When I first came to Canada, my goals were to gain both independence from my parents and international experience. When you are setting your goals, they must be *your* goals. They shouldn't be your parents' goals or your friends' goals. The only way you will be passionate about achieving these goals is if they are your own.

Your goals are a major part of the blueprint of your future. You don't succeed by accident, and things will not simply be handed to you. You will need to work for them.

Let me tell you a story about how I came up with some of my early goals shortly after arriving in Canada.

When Things Go Bad

When I say I know the fear and trepidation you are feeling, I am talking from personal experience. It was not only the fear of leaving home. Even after I arrived, there were many incidents that upset me and threatened to derail my dream. I've already talked about the store manager who did not want to speak to me because I was an international student. That was enough to get me down, but, just a short time later, I had another terrible experience.

A family friend who had come to Canada to study told her Canadian boyfriend that I had been flirting with her, which was not true at all. However, that did not go over well with her boyfriend, who happened to be in a gang. He and his friends hunted me down and threatened me, essentially telling me that I was very "colourful" and all, but that I had to "get the f*** out of the country." As you can imagine, I was scared and devastated. I felt betrayed, and then I had to get back to school. I was upset and crying, and I did not want to tell anyone what had happened, especially that I had run away from a fight.

After I returned to school, I realized I had some choices to make. I could tuck my tail between my legs and quit, or I could persevere and become the person that I always wanted to be. The fact that you are reading this book right now tells you that I chose the latter. That day, I made a commitment to myself.

I started to write down my goals—the things that were most important to me.

I want to be fluent in English.
I want to make Canadian friends.
I want to graduate from high school with distinction.
I want to go to the top university.
I want to make my parents proud.
I want to make an impact in this world.

And, I wanted to do all of that in a year. Sure, that might sound like a lot, but these were *my* goals. Since I had a strong desire, clarity, and a sense of purpose, I had a lot of motivation.

My English improved since I chose to speak only in English with everyone except my family. I lost some friends, which was fine, since they did not support my dreams and goals and therefore were not real friends. Since I went outside my comfort zone to speak English, I started relating more to Canadians. As I spoke more English, I also started to better understand the material in my classes and I no longer had to translate word for word from English to Russian. I became more confident and my grades improved significantly, which resulted in me graduating with distinction. With great grades, I got into a top university which made my parents proud. Since I became a better person, I made a positive impact on my family, which is the best way to make this world a better place.

Let's look at a few goal-setting tips to help you get started.

Goal-Setting Tips

If you want to set powerful goals, make sure they are relevant to *you*. You should be passionate, even obsessed about these goals.

Evaluate your life right now. Reflect on who you are and what you want to be. Set goals that match your dreams, and make sure your goals are SMART. What do I mean by this? It's simple. Let's break down the acronym.

SMART—Specific, Measurable, Attainable, Realistic, Time-Sensitive

- **Specific:** Be clear about what you want to achieve.
- **Measurable:** Make sure that you can quantify your goal. You have to be able to measure it, so you know when you have achieved it.
- **Attainable:** Be honest about what you can attain at this point in your life.
- **Realistic:** Make sure the goals are practical and doable.
- **Time-Sensitive:** Set a timeframe to achieve your goals. Remember, I gave myself a timeframe of one year.

If you want to achieve your goals, you also need to be willing to hold yourself accountable for those times when you are not as focused as you should be. You may be able to find someone willing to hold you responsible, but ultimately, you cannot shift the blame onto them. The responsibility rests with you. Surrounding yourself with mentors, coaches, friends, and positive influences can help you strive harder to reach your goals.

Whenever you are feeling down or like you want to quit, think about how far you have already come and the possibilities that lie ahead. Even if the goals are relatively new to you, focus on your intended outcome rather than on what will happen if you fail. Strive to stay positive, and make sure you check regularly to see how you are progressing.

Whether you want to improve your English skills, make some new friends by joining a club that interests you, or get into the perfect program for the career you want to pursue, remember that you can do it. Create these workable goals and push yourself toward them. Before long, you will start to see little successes that will spur you on to even larger achievements.

"But, Boris, I Don't Know What I Want!"

This is a fair statement. Ultimately, we all want happiness in life. What is happiness?

It is not the achievement of goals. It is the journey towards achieving these goals. While I surely enjoy experiencing a sense of accomplishment, as I will, for example, when I finish writing this book, what makes me most happy is what I am learning along the way about the process of writing and publishing a book. Learning makes me happy.

I believe that happiness is the ultimate currency of success. In his book, *Happier: Learn the Secrets to Daily Joy and Lasting Fulfillment*, author Tal Ben-Shahar defines happiness as the overall feeling of pleasure and meaning. He writes, "Happiness is not about making it to the peak of the mountain, nor is it about climbing aimlessly around the mountain, happiness is the experience of climbing toward the peak."

If you look deep inside yourself, I am sure you can identify things in your life you enjoy doing and which are meaningful to you and people around you. If you are not certain, that's fine. You just need to start the journey. Society and parents put pressure on us to know exactly what we want, but this is not realistic. Humans are emotional creatures, and we need time to discover our passions, strengths, and purpose in life.

In order to experience a sense of purpose, "the goals we set for ourselves need to be intrinsically meaningful," says Tal Ben-Shahar. Embark on a journey to discover happiness in your life though purposeful goals.

Exercise: Start Setting Goals Now

Why wait to set your goals? The perfect time to take out a piece of paper or a Post-It note and start writing is right now. Use the tips in this chapter to formulate your goals. Then, look for ways that you can make those goals actionable. Write down how you can start to get closer to reaching those goals. Use the SMART acronym to guide you and find ways that you can work toward your goals each day.

Chapter 4: How and Where to Get Answers to Your Questions

"Research is formalized curiosity. It is poking and prying with a purpose." – Zora Neale Hurston

Keep learning about Canada and the schools you are going to apply to. Try to find out as much information as you can. Write down any questions and make sure you look for answers. It does not matter how large or small those questions might seem. If they are important to you, they are important. Talk with people online, read more about the location, and watch videos. Truly immerse yourself in the new culture *before* you arrive.

The questions you ask should go well beyond just the culture and geography of Canada, of course. You will have to ask how you will support yourself while you are there. How will you communicate with your family? What will you be doing about holidays when the school is closed? Will you be staying on campus, in a homestay, or renting an apartment?

As you start learning, you will find you have more and more questions. Write them down and then find answers—by yourself, or from your family, education agents, faculty and staff at the school you are considering, alumni, etc. Stay curious and keep asking questions. It will help demystify every step of the process. This book is a great start but keep going.

In this chapter, we will look at some of the resources where you will find the most pertinent information.

Do Your Research

One of the biggest mistakes that some prospective students make is not doing enough research. Those students might not have thought about, for example, financial support beyond their savings and what their parents are able to give them. Perhaps they don't know enough about the city where they will be living, or they might not have acquainted themselves with local customs and laws.

The less prepared you are, the more difficult this massive transition will be. I promise you. There is a saying that failing to plan is planning to fail, and that's very true. If you don't put in the effort right now to start learning more about the country and city where you will be staying, if you don't practice your language skills, and if you don't have your finances in order, you will certainly be stressed out.

Though, be cautious about paralysis by analysis. This is when you conduct way too much research and feel overwhelmed with information. You need just enough information to feel confident and informed about the decisions you are making. I have met many families who have consulted with me and other professionals, but at some point in their research, they have become overwhelmed with information and advice and, as a result, they've taken no action to lift their lives to the next level. The problem is that they are not asking the right questions and are just collecting information.

In her book *Prepared: What Kids Need for a Fulfilled Life*, author Diana Tavenner explains that being prepared for schooling means having self-direction, a sense of purpose, and curiosity. When you study abroad, you are self-directing your future. When you do things which are meaningful to you and that you are passionate about, you have a sense of purpose. When you do your research and ask the right questions, you are curious. Developing these habits will prepare you for success in your studies and life.

Reach Out to People to Get More Information

There are many international students who are going through school in Canada right now. There are many more people who have done it in the past, as I have. There is a world of information out there, but it is not going to be handed to you. Sometimes, you need to do the footwork and make contact with people who can help.

Perhaps you know people online who live in Canada. If you don't, they can easily be found on social media. You can talk with education agents who help place students. You can find articles and videos on YouTube to learn more about all aspects of living and getting an education in Canada.

People love helping others, especially when you do some initial research yourself, prepare thoughtful questions, and make them feel they are an expert in whatever area you are interested in learning more about.

Agents

Education agents are companies or individuals who provide support and placement services to students who want to study overseas. The purpose of the agent is to advise you and your parents when selecting a school, a program of study, and a destination. They can be a fantastic source of up to date information. Some agents are highly specialized while others will have a broad level of knowledge.

While you may be able to find a school and apply without an agent, it is often easier to have someone to help guide you through the process and answer the questions that you and your parents are sure to have.

There are many agents who offer these services. However, it is important to note that the Government of Canada does not qualify, accredit, or endorse any agent or company. Therefore, you should research the background of any agent you are considering. Ask your friends for references. Ask any agent you approach which institutions in Canada authorize their services. Make sure that whoever you plan to work with is the right choice for you and a good fit.

A good agent will have a wealth of information regarding the schools and the provinces and cities where they are located. They can be a very good resource when you are just starting to plan, but they may be of equal assistance once you have arrived and started school. Make sure to ask tough questions to test the agent's knowledge, level of motivation, passion, professionalism, ethics, etc. There are many exceptional agents, but also a few bad apples out there.

I was very fortunate to work with an agent who helped with my high school and first visa applications to Canada. However, I did all future school, visa, immigration, and citizenship applications on my own.

Fairs

There are numerous educational fairs organized by agencies, specialized fair organizers, or Canadian Embassies worldwide where you can learn more about studying abroad, and in Canada in particular. At these fairs, you will meet school representatives based in your region and recruiters from Canada who have made the trip to meet you in person. If you plan to attend a fair, research participating schools and come prepared with questions.

You can visit the Canadian government website Educanada.ca, which provides information on studying abroad, getting international scholarships, finding programs, costs, and more. The trade section of the Canadian embassy or high commission in your country is another place to look.

School Representatives and Faculty

Remember that your choices are not limited to schools you've heard about at educational fairs; you are free to apply to any school you desire. It could be a school that a friend or family member told you about. It could be one you found online. When your list has been finalized, visit websites to find out more about your choices. When you've found out all you can there, especially if you still have questions, it's time to contact the various school representatives and faculty.

School representatives such as recruitment and admissions officers can provide you with additional information on their school, the programs offered, housing, and more. Faculty, on the other hand, should be able to answer specific questions regarding programs, classes and research activities.

Here is a list of some of the things that you will want to research and ask, but feel free to add your questions to the list.

- What's the graduation rate and the rate of employment of international students?
- What support is offered to international students before and during the program and after graduation?
- What types of facilities for international students are available on campus?
- How safe is the campus for international students?
- Are there dedicated academic support services for international students?

- Are there dedicated career services for international students?
- What leadership opportunities are available?
- What accommodations are available to students on and off campus?

Alumni

Alumni can be another great source of information. It is a good idea to contact recent graduates as they will be able to give you an up to date idea of exactly what to expect when you arrive at school. Social media is a very good place to find these contacts.

Many schools will generally have a presence on Facebook with groups for alumni. If you're lucky, one of those groups might be in your home community. LinkedIn makes it possible to find alumni from certain schools as well. Direct your questions to appropriate alumni. For example, if you are going into a science program, you may not want to ask specifics about science courses from someone who graduated in business. Focus your search. Prepare your questions in advance.

While preparing my university application, I depended upon Facebook and LinkedIn to establish connections with current students, alumni, and representatives from my desired schools. These connections not only helped me get insider information on the schools and determine cultural fit, but also follow and engage with them as I progressed in life. You never know when a connection will come in handy for you, or when you will be resourceful for another person in their life journey.

Exercise: Start a List of Potential Contacts

There is no time like the present to get started on this purposeful research. Go to the websites of the various schools you are considering and make a list of the relevant agents, representatives and faculty and their contact information. Take time to search some social media sites for groups attached to the schools that you are considering. Make sure you organize your findings.

Once you have your lists ready, you can then start to make contact based on the schools that most interest you. Find answers to your questions. This will help you focus your plans and identify your top choices.

Treat every contact as you would like to be treated and remember that every connection brings you closer to your goals and dreams.

Chapter 5: How to Choose a School/Program

"May your choices reflect your hopes, not your fears."
– Nelson Mandela

Choosing a school and a program of specialization is not always easy. Knowing exactly what you want to do with the rest of your life and knowing the career path you should take is challenging to say the least.

Many international students and their parents will have trouble when it comes to understanding a foreign education system and the myriad of career options available. Sometimes, there is simply too much information. In addition, there is often pressure from parents, not to mention generational and market differences.

We've all heard stories of parents who want their children to become doctors or lawyers, and then push them hard in that direction. This rarely works well, and most of the time, the student rebels.

My parents wanted me to study engineering. It took a lot of convincing before they understood that my passion is in marketing and that it offered better career opportunities after graduation. I asked myself some tough questions which helped me gain clarity and focus before I made my case to them.

Listen to Your Heart and Your Intuition

You may feel you are facing the unknown, and I know how frightening that can be. You will miss your family, friends, and the life that you currently have in your home country. However, you have to think about your future. You have to think about what you want and develop a vision of where you see yourself in the short and long term. If you want more opportunities, applying to schools is the first step. Just make sure that you do not let fear be the driving force. We've all been afraid before and we will be afraid again of something new in our lives.

To overcome fear, you need momentum in what you are doing. With momentum, you gain confidence and become unstoppable. In order to gain confidence, you have to program yourself to visualize and believe in the future result right now.

Put this book aside and answer the following questions before you continue:

1. What are you good at?
2. What could you be the best at?
3. What makes you happy?
4. What excites you?
5. What makes you feel accomplished and good about yourself?

6. What are the accomplishments you are most proud of?
7. Can you repeat these and further develop them?
8. What do you enjoy sharing and experiencing with others?

You can download a workbook to help guide you through these questions at **StartRightBook.com/resources.**

How to Read Rankings

Canada is home to more than 20 of the top 500 universities in the world according to the Times Higher Education's World University Rankings. There are a number of excellent schools in Canada, but this does not mean they are all right for your needs. When looking at the rankings of schools, check to see how the rankings are calculated. In some instances, the rankings are based on opinions. In other cases, they take into account measurable factors such as:

- Academic reputation
- Student body characteristics
- Class sizes and faculty-to-student ratio
- Citation per faculty
- Library resources
- Specialization expertise
- Student options
- Graduate employment

Different lists and rankings will prioritize different factors. Therefore, you need to understand exactly what each set of listings is based on. In fact, only universities are consistently and systematically ranked, while language schools, high schools, and colleges are generally not. Rankings are useful when weighing the decision of where to apply, but I encourage you to develop your own ranking system, with factors relevant to you such as location, culture, perceived value, etc.

Location, Location, Location!

Where is the school you are interested in located? Canada is a large country, and some of its largest cities are very far apart and quite different from one another. Each one has its own personality and style, and this can be important when you are making your decision.

Naturally, you want to choose a school that can provide the best education possible. However, you also want to be in a safe location and one that offers a lot from a cultural perspective. Do you prefer a large city or a small one? Are you interested in a city where the majority of the people speak French? Do you like to hike, bike, and ski in your spare time? Do you want to live near the ocean or in the north? Fortunately, you will be able to find a great school in a great city, no matter what your needs are.

Assess Fit

It is also important to ensure you feel the school is a proper fit. This means that you want the school to match what you need at an academic level. However, it also needs to be in a location that will work for you. That might mean you need to think about what's affordable.

Both the school and its location should be able to help you stay on track when it comes to your chosen path.

Think about the things you believe you "must have" from a school and try to get a better sense of just what it would be like to go to school at your desired location. If you have the capability, visit the campus before you commit. This will let you and your parents get a better understanding of the school and what you can anticipate when you arrive there.

You might also consider interviewing the school to make sure they are a good fit. After all, when you are deciding where to apply and where to go, you are in the driver's seat. If you are lucky and have several schools that accept you, then you can be selective.

Regardless of how many options you have, whether it is one or half a dozen, you want to learn everything that you can about the school(s). Interview the representatives as if they are the ones applying to you. Remember, you will be committing a lot of time and money to this school. This is a two-way interview process and you have a right to ask tough questions. For example, you can ask, "If I am fortunate to receive an offer to your school, why should I NOT attend?"

Don't Take Anything at Face Value

Although you may want to believe the things you are told by the agents, school officials and representatives, and others who are trying to get you to go to their school, you should not take everyone at their word. Sometimes, people will give you misinformation by mistake. Sometimes the information they offer is out of date. Other people will not be honest because they want your business so badly, they have no problem being deceptive.

When people and organizations offer information about your schooling, the accommodations, your future, etc., you shouldn't take them at face value. This is true whether they say something you want to hear or not. Just because they give you what you feel is good news does not mean it is honest news.

You need to research and confirm what they have said. Also, if someone were to make promises about getting into a program or a residence that you want, etc., you would need to get those promises and offers in writing. This will provide you with some assurance that they will be able to back up their promises.

I have seen countless times when international students were misled because they did not perform their own due diligence on the information provided by agents, schools, etc. There are people who are only out to make money on international students. This can be an expensive mistake if you don't verify the information yourself. It is your future and you are responsible for the choices you make.

Take Your Time to Ensure You Make the Right Decision

The right school for one person might not fit the next. Parents often put a lot of emphasis on getting into top-ranked schools, just as they do on establishing a stable career with a dream company. While these are great achievements, and they might make you happy for a time, they need to be what *you want*. If you don't create a plan for yourself, your parents or someone else will. Avoid this.

If you are not in love with the school or program that you choose, the novelty of being in a foreign country will wear off very quickly. It's at that point that disappointment and dissatisfaction start to set in, and you start to think you've made a colossal mistake.

Therefore, you need to make sure both that you understand what you want and that you are proactive in finding it. Take a holistic approach. Be aware of what your needs are when you are choosing a school, when you are at school, and for the rest of your life. Understanding what you need and striving to meet those needs will make you happier than if you follow a path put forth by someone else.

Exercise: Time to Start Your School Decision Matrix

Choosing between schools can be extremely difficult. Even when you do plenty of research, there is sometimes conflicting information about which schools are best depending on the criteria that you use. Using a decision matrix can be a fantastic way of comparing schools and putting all the most important criteria right up front. This way, you will be able to make a sound decision.

Creating a decision matrix is simple. First, list each school's name down the left side of a piece of paper or on a digital spreadsheet, such as in Excel. List the criteria you are looking for across the top of the sheet. Think about the most important criteria and prioritize them on your list. These might include things like net price, programs available, location, etc. Then make notes about what that school has to offer. Keep adding schools as you find new options. Remove schools as soon as you see they will not meet your needs.

When you're done, all the important information will be on a single sheet. By starting your matrix now, you will find you have time to get all the information you need. When you are ready to start applying, the matrix will help you focus first on your ideal schools.

Head over to **StartRightBook.com/resources** to download a sample decision matrix.

Chapter 6: How to Fund Your Studies

"An investment in knowledge pays the best interest." –
Benjamin Franklin

In addition to finding the right school to put you on the path to success, you will also need to make sure you and your parents can afford the school fees. It is essential also to consider the overall cost of living while you are in Canada. You must have your financial affairs in order.

The following are some of the different ways you can get money to take care of your expenses while you are in school.

Savings

One of the most important sources of money is your savings. Your parents may have been saving money for your schooling, for example, and this money can be used to supplement other options discussed in this chapter. Of course, many families do not have massive savings. Fortunately, there are other methods of getting the money needed for your tuition and personal expenses while you are away.

Scholarships

One of the best ways to take care of a substantial amount of program costs is to attempt to get a scholarship. You can speak to the financial aid department of the schools that interest you, and they can often point you in the right direction. Remember to research financial aid for prospective and current students at every school you are applying to as the results may be quite different.

For example, through the relationships I built at my high school and universities, I was awarded thousands of dollars in scholarships. While I met the merit requirements for these awards, it is the genuine relationships which I formed with the faculty and staff that played a key role in getting financial aid and recognition for my accomplishments.

Although there are many students who want to study abroad, not everyone has the means. However, as author Tony Robbins says, it is not the lack of *resources*, it is the lack of *resourcefulness* that stops people from pursuing their dreams. In my first year in business school, I discovered that there were no scholarships for current international students who assumed leadership positions. So, I decided to create one. I did a lot of lobbying, and I went through the bureaucratic process to establish the International Student Leadership Scholarship at the Sauder School of Business at the University of British Columbia. While my objective was to have it established for all current and future students, I knew that I, too, might benefit from this scholarship, as long I met the criteria. Unfortunately, by the time it passed through the university approvals process, I had already graduated. However, I was very happy the day I got to award this inaugural scholarship to a fellow international student.

Giving back has always been an important part of my life, and as an avid traveller, I created a Remes Family Study Abroad Scholarship which provided a ticket to a study abroad destination for Canadian students. Canadians will also immensely benefit from being international students abroad.

Head over to **StartRightBook.com/resources** to find additional information on scholarships.

Employment During Studies

Another great option that will help supplement your finances is to find a job. While getting an education is the reason you are in Canada in the first place, getting a job to support your needs can help in a host of ways.

Not only will you receive your paycheque, which you can then put toward your cost of living, but you will also be gaining Canadian work experience. You will be able to learn more about the culture, you will meet new people and make new contacts, and you will feel like you are a full-fledged and contributing member of the society in which you now reside.

When choosing a job, make sure it does not interfere with your schooling. A part-time job for 15 to 20 hours a week can bring in some much-needed money, but it should not come at the expense of your academic success. Remember to check the conditions of your visa.

I started my first company just two months into my undergraduate degree, and it was a great way to earn some cash and get Canadian experience. You can work either for yourself or for someone else.

Loan Programs

You will also want to look into loan programs. You or your parents might be able to get a personal loan in your home country, which could be used to pay for your schooling. You may also find that some colleges and universities offer international students a one-time emergency loan. Talk with the school's financial aid department to see what might be available.

Unfortunately, international students who have study permits are not eligible for bank or government student loans in Canada. However, those who plan to apply for permanent resident status could be eligible for these types of loans once the status has been granted. You will need a good credit history to qualify, which we will discuss in subsequent chapters. This can be very helpful when planning further studies.

Exercise: Create a Budget

Even if you don't plan to apply to a school for a year or two, there is no harm in starting to put together a budget. I have provided you with a template on

StartRightBook.com/resources. Sources of income, program costs, and expected costs of living in your desired location will all be important to planning your budget. The websites of some universities and colleges may provide information about the cost of living in their cities.

Also, do your research into scholarships as early as possible. Use the web, resources from the schools and their faculty, etc. to start a list of scholarships that could fill your needs. Keep researching to look for new or overlooked scholarships or grants that might be available as the time to apply draws closer. Even a relatively small scholarship of a few thousand dollars can help offset your costs substantially. But keep track of all application deadlines.

Chapter 7: Applying to Your School

At this point, you should have done plenty of research on the schools that match your needs. You should have found schools that will be affordable and that you believe you can get into. Don't fall into the trap of thinking that you should only apply to the biggest and best schools in the country. There are plenty of great schools and applying to several is more strategic than just picking your one or two favourites.

How to Apply

There are two ways to go about applying to a school in Canada. First, you can apply directly to the school. To learn how, you will need to go to the school's website, and you may need to contact someone from the school if you have any questions about application requirements.

There is also the option of going through an agent. Working with an agent, as mentioned earlier, can make things much easier. They can explain everything that needs to be done and the paperwork you will need to have. They are the link between you and the school. Some agents have physical offices in your country, while others may be based entirely online.

There are many excellent benefits to using an agent:

- They strive to understand your needs and goals.
- They can suggest schools and programs that will help you reach those goals.
- They can help gather documents needed for the application process.
- They can guide you through the application process.
- They can help to prepare for the move and the arrival.
- Some agents can help with arranging pickup from the airport and accommodation.

These are some of the many reasons that people today choose agents. Even though there is a cost for their services, a good agent is worth the money. They can make the entire application process smoother in most cases. However, once you are at your school, you should be able to stand on your own two feet. You do not want to be overly reliant on the agent. This will be the time for you to shine.

Ultimately, you can choose the route you and your parents find most comfortable, whether it is applying on your own or working with an education agent.

What You Need to Apply

The documentation that you need when applying can vary based on where you will be studying. However, you will find that the following types of documents will be required in most circumstances. Make sure you have all of these in order before you start if you are applying on your own. If you are working with an agent, they may be able to help you gather the documents you need. Generally, you will need:

- Transcripts of your grades
- Proof of language skills. Accepted tests typically include the Test of English as a Foreign Language (TOEFL), International English Language Testing System (IELTS), and the Canadian Academic English Language Assessment (CAEL)
- Admissions essays
- References

How Your Application is Evaluated

Some Canadian university programs utilize rolling admissions, which means that after your application has been received, they will be able to evaluate it and make a decision. There are also competitive admissions, in which the application is not evaluated until a deadline has passed and all applications have been received. These types of admissions evaluations will take longer.

However, you may be wondering just what criteria are used when the university does the evaluation and determines whether to make you an offer or not. Naturally, they are going to look at your transcripts, as well as essays to help them determine whether you would make a good fit for their school. I'd like to impart a secret as an admissions decision maker myself: it's important to build up a relationship and rapport with the school and the people who are going to be making these determinations. You will want to learn to tell your story in writing and in person. If you can attend events (online or in-person) before you apply and get the business cards and names of the people who work in admissions and who will be making the decisions, you will find that when you are honest and sincere, grades are not the only deciding factor.

Choose the Best Offer

After you have applied, the wait to find out whether you have been accepted can be agonizing. It might take just a week or two, or it could take much longer, depending on how the school does their admissions. Sooner or later, though, you will start to get responses. It can be nerve-wracking when they arrive by email or via post.

If you are fortunate, you will have found a school that will accept you. If you are *extremely* lucky, you might have several schools that are vying for your loyalty. Provided you were diligent about choosing the schools in the first place, you can be relatively sure these would all be a good fit for you.

However, now that you have actual options and offers before you, it's time to make your decision. It's one of the biggest decisions of your life, too, so you will want to make sure that you give it the full weight it deserves. This means going back over the pros and cons of the different schools, so you can identify the one that will be perfect for the path you want to follow. Review your decision matrix. Is there anything you need to revise or add now? While making your final decision, don't forget to listen to your heart and intuition.

Apply for a Visa

Although you can hire people to help with the process of getting a student visa, you will find that it's easily manageable. I did it myself many times after the initial student visa application, and you can do the same. The first thing you must do is visit Canada.ca and check the page on immigration and citizenship. This will provide you with the information you need to get a study permit. This permit is technically not a visa, but it lets foreign nationals study at designated learning institutions in Canada. Depending on where you are from, you might require a Temporary Resident Visa (TRV) to enter Canada, so make sure to check.

Exercise: Prepare Your Documentation

There's no such thing as getting started too early. Even before you apply, get your paperwork and documentation in order. Prepare for your first encounter with an agent, if that's the way you choose to go, by thinking about the information you need and gathering your questions well before the meeting. It will make the process flow smoothly, and you won't have to run around at the last minute trying to find everything you need. As it is in all domains, a good plan here will keep you on the right track.

Chapter 8: Arriving in Canada

"One of the greatest discoveries a man makes, one of his great surprises, is to find he can do what he was afraid he couldn't do." – Henry Ford

As the time to leave your home and make your way to Canada and your new school grows closer, there is a lot to consider and do to make sure you bring everything that you need along with you. This is the time to prepare what you need to pack, say goodbye to family and friends, and start setting your goals.

Leaving behind family and friends is hard. I know that, for me, this was challenging. Growing up, I made good friends, just as you have likely done. My parents were very caring, supportive, and brave. After all, not all parents would agree to send their child to Canada on a one-way ticket.

They trusted my choice and knew that the opportunities were too good to pass up. I knew this too. Leaving was difficult, but it was the best thing for me. It gave me opportunities that I would not have had otherwise.

I want to make your transition to Canada as easy as possible, so I wrote this chapter to help you develop a good understanding of what you need to bring with you.

Pack

Packing for Canada as an international student is different from packing for a vacation. You need to have a number of essential items. These include your documentation, discussed further in the next section. You should also make it a point to take between $100 and $200 in cash with you. This will be enough money to last for several days until you can get settled and find an ATM. Credit cards issued in your home country will also be widely accepted and are safer than carrying cash.

If you have glasses or contact lenses, make sure you remember to pack them, as well as a spare pair or set. Don't forget the mobile chargers for your phone, laptop, tablet, and other devices. Of course, you need to make sure you remember to pack those devices, as well. You don't want to end up in Canada only to realize that your laptop charger is still sitting on the dresser in your parents' home! This happened to me. Use the list that's on the Start Right website, but also check out other lists—your new school may provide one on its website—to see if there is anything you've overlooked. Make your own additions to the list, as needed.

Go to **StartRightBook.com/resources** to access a list of recommended items.

Remember just how cold it gets in Canada in winter. When you are packing clothing, make sure to account for the weather. Sure, there are some warm sunny days, but there are some very cold and snowy ones as well, especially in certain parts of Canada. Pack warm clothing and be ready to buy other warm items after you arrive.

Now that you have a better idea of what you will need to pack, you must not wait until the last minute to gather these things. Start early and double-check, and then *triple-check* to make sure you have everything.

Double Check Your Documentation

When you arrive in Canada, you will need to have more than just your luggage if you want to get into the country. Do not make the mistake of forgetting important paperwork that you will need when you arrive. If you are working with an agent, he or she may be able to help ensure you have assembled all the right documents.

Keep those documents with you, along with any other valuable papers, cash, etc. Do not put them into your checked luggage. If any documentation were to go missing, you would not be allowed to enter Canada. Keep the paperwork on your person and check to make sure you have everything before you leave for the airport.

If you decide to travel outside Canada, such as to the United States for a short vacation, make sure you have your passport, study permit, and Canadian and US visas (if applicable) with you, so you can get back into the country.

Exercise: Find and Face Your Fear

It can be difficult to face a big fear. It can be just as difficult to face small fears. In this exercise, I encourage you to consider some of the things that make you afraid or anxious and then attempt to face down those fears.

Start with a small fear. Maybe you do not like speaking in public, for example. The goal is to face that fear and overcome it, so you know that it is possible. You will find that even though you were afraid, you made it through to the other side. If you fail the first time, keep trying. It is a process and even though you feel like you are not moving ahead, you are taking small steps internally. Eventually, if you keep trying, you should be able to face down your fear. But it is okay to fail. It happens and it doesn't mean you should give up.

Having a few successes with small fears will put you into a mindset where you are more willing to try to conquer large fears. When you do this, you will start to see that facing down the fear of moving overseas to study is very doable. If you need to get over a few small fears first, that is fine. You are becoming a stronger person because of it.

Here are the steps:

1. Write down one of the things you are afraid of.
2. Create a step to help you get over this fear.
3. Determine when you are going to take this step.
4. Take the step and reward yourself.

Chapter 9: The First 90 Days

The first three months you spend in Canada are likely going to be the hardest. Everything will be new, and while that is exciting, it can also be frightening. Even with all the research you have done on the school and the city where you will be living, you will find there is a big difference when it comes to *being there* and experiencing it firsthand.

This chapter offers a crash course in what I believe are the most important things to do during your first 90 days in Canada. This is going to be a big chapter, and it will feel like there's a lot you have to do. That's because there is. Not only will the tips and techniques in this chapter help you to fit in and better assimilate, but they will also make sure you are kept busy and that you are making headway toward your goals.

When I first arrived, I felt excited and fortunate. I was looking forward to exploring the area I was living in, learning about different cultures, and seeing what this new world held for me. Of course, I had my worries. I was worried about making new friends. I was also worried about learning English, settling in, getting good grades, and staying healthy.

No one will be there to hold your hand. If you want to succeed now, you have to be willing to do the legwork. I know that it will be hard. I've been there. I also know that it will be well worth it. When you get through those first 90 days, you will have more self-confidence. You will learn that with the right planning and work, you can reach your goals.

What Habits Do You Need to Succeed in the First 90 Days?

Developing good habits in those first 90 days will help improve your chance of success. You will find that even though there are many habits to adopt, they will quickly become second nature. You will need to remind yourself regularly not only of your goals but also of the things you need to do to reach those goals.

The first 90 days are crucial when it comes to forming new habits. You will start to develop both good and bad habits. You must be aware of any bad habits that creep their way into your life. For example, eating unhealthy food and overeating, not getting enough sleep, taking drugs and drinking alcohol, spending too much time socializing and not enough time studying and working toward your goals: recognize the bad habits and make it a point to stop them before they become too difficult to break.

Do what it takes to instill good habits and traits into your daily life.

Put First Things First

What are the most important things to do when you first arrive in the country? The following suggestions are things you will want to take care of as soon as you can. Each of these will make life easier in a range of ways and help you fit in more comfortably.

Attend Orientation

Attend your new school's orientation and be engaged in what is happening. It is a chance for new students to understand how everything works at their school and to meet other students. You will be able to meet faculty and staff during most orientations. The orientation can lead to a much smoother transition and make you feel more comfortable about the amount of independence you now have.

Get Your Accommodation in Order

Your accommodation, whether on or off campus, will be your home while you are schooling. Therefore, set it up nicely. Unpack and put away your belongings. If you have a roommate, make sure you understand each other. State your expectations about noise levels, guests, cleanliness, and so on, but be prepared to compromise. Your roommate is likely to be one of the first friends that you make, and you must be respectful of one another's time and space.

Items You Need

Once you've unpacked and settled into your new accommodation, you might find there are still a few things you need. It might be some food, a SIM card, a better pillow, or an additional blanket, for example. You might need to stock up on toiletries and grooming supplies. You may be able to find what you need at a store on campus, or you might need to venture off campus. Ask your roommate or another friend to go with you, both so you have some company and so you feel a bit safer venturing out in those early days. Eventually, you will get used to heading out on your own, of course. You can also save a lot of money on furniture, appliances, books, etc., by getting them second-hand on Craigslist, Kijiji, Let Go, or another website where people list items for sale.

Set Up a Bank Account and Get a Credit Card

Open a bank account and pay your tuition and fees. Get a credit card and an ATM card if you do not already have them. You can use the credit card to start slowly building your credit history, which will be helpful later when you want to get a mortgage or loan. Of course, you must be disciplined with your finances, especially with your credit card. Just because you are given a high credit limit does not mean you have to use it. Be careful and make sure you pay your credit card bills on time and in full otherwise it can ruin your credit rating. You will thank me later when you get your first mortgage, car, or business loan.

Head over to **StartRightBook.com/resources** to see recommended bank accounts and credit cards for international students.

Public Transportation

If you are going to be taking public transportation in the Greater Toronto and Hamilton Area, or in Ottawa, get a PRESTO Card. The card is an electronic payment system that makes travelling on transit faster and easier. It eliminates the need for tickets, passes, tokens, or cash. When you buy the card, you load it with cash, and each time you use the card, the fare is automatically deducted from the balance on your card. When the balance on the card runs out, you again reload it with cash at a vending machine or online. Other metropolitan areas in Canada also have reloadable cards to access public transit, such as Compass in Vancouver and Opus in Montreal. Ask if there is a reloadable card in your new city, and, if there's not, ask about monthly and annual passes that might also get you a discounted fare.

Driving in Canada

Most international students who come to Canada are eligible to drive. However, it will depend on both your driving history in your previous country as well as the rules in the province where you are studying. Even if you have a valid foreign licence, you may find it advantageous to get a Canadian driver's licence.

Before you arrive, look up the requirements and regulations for the province where you will be studying.

Search for "Driving in Canada" on Canada.ca where you will find information for international drivers. Then, if you decide you want a Canadian licence, you will have to take a test after you arrive.

Before you take your test, make sure you learn the rules of the road in the province where you are going to school. If you are going to buy a vehicle, you will need to register it and purchase insurance to protect yourself and others.

Deal with Culture Shock

Culture shock is something that all international students experience when they come to Canada. It's an entirely new world, and even if you have visited Canada before, there is a big difference between visiting and living here.

I had never been to the country before, so the only thing I had to go by was the research I had done. While that was helpful, there were still surprises. It is those first three months and how you deal with these changes that can make a difference in whether you succeed or fail.

Many things can cause culture shock. It's not just being in an unknown environment. Culturally, you sense the absence of many things you have been surrounded by your entire life. For example, you hear different languages being spoken, and you see new landscapes. The food tastes different. There is not enough spice or not enough avocados around. The air in your room smells different. Your body feels different because of the temperature. Winter is coming. There is also the shock of different academic and professional expectations. You may feel the pressure of readings, assignments, papers, and midterms. Perhaps the culture around education and learning is different from where you grew up. But you need to find a way to fit in.

Remember that shock is an impermanent state. You will eventually adapt. Balance is the key. Your body is craving your old, comfortable lifestyle, and expressing aversion toward new challenges.

At this time, you will feel a natural attraction towards your cultural group which can offer you a lot of the comforts that will satisfy your needs, such as language, common interests, and food. You will find yourself gravitating toward this group. However, you can look at your newness to the country and culture as something of an advantage. You are getting a fresh start, and you can start building your reputation from the ground up. You can become the person you want to be. This does not mean you have to give up your culture. Of course not. Spend some time with your cultural group but do not forget to venture out and try new experiences, too.

Immerse yourself as soon as possible. But be proud of who you are and your background. Adjust your expectations and stay authentic.

Avoid the Cultural Bubble

A cultural bubble is something that many people, not merely international students, inadvertently enter. Essentially a cultural bubble is a place where you can be among people who share your beliefs, values, and opinions, while you cut yourself off from other ways of looking at the world. Sometimes people will only socialize with others from the same country or part of the world they are from. While there is nothing wrong with making friends from your own country, you should make sure you do not end up in a cultural bubble where you only associate with them and other international students.

If you stay in the bubble, a comfort zone for many people, you will not grow. You need to expand your horizons and develop your unique point of view. Spend time with different people. Join clubs and take on leadership roles. Remember that bubbles only have a certain amount of air in them. Don't let a cultural bubble suffocate you.

Learn the Cultural Norms

It's important that as you start to immerse yourself in Canadian culture, you start to take note of how most people do things. For example, you should not start a conversation about politics or religion until you know someone really well, and perhaps wait until they initiate it. You probably should not ever discuss your parents' wealth (or lack of), body scent, and similar topics. Be aware that you also need to provide people with a good amount of personal space. Getting too close when you are speaking often makes people in Canada feel uncomfortable, even though it might be normal in your culture.

As a cultural norm, it is disrespectful to ask how much money someone makes or discuss your salary. Many individuals who are married and live together do not even disclose how much they make to their significant other.

Canadians are generally considered to be very polite. You will want to mirror this politeness. When you are wrong or when you bump into them, etc., you will want to say you are sorry. Furthermore, you will always want to wait in line until it is your turn. Many Canadians frown on queue jumping, and if you want to find out how much they dislike the practice, try it one day and see what happens.

Keep in mind that you also never really know who speaks your language. I made this mistake. I was on the bus and upset, and I started swearing at the bus driver in my native tongue. It turned out that he understood what I was saying. The driver got extremely upset and kicked me off the bus. Also, even though people might not be able to understand your exact words, they can often understand the intent. When you are upset and swearing, this can paint you, and all international students, in a negative light.

Learn English Fast

I have talked about the importance of learning and polishing your English, and I want to stress the significance here. Learning to speak English clearly, and learning to understand what is spoken to you will help in your schooling, your ability to make new friends, with your jobs, and simply with communicating when you travel. Language is a barrier that is relatively easy to tear down, provided you put in the work and learn.

You have likely been learning and practicing in your own country, but you need to do more. Do not just take a single English language course and think you are proficient enough to manage in Canada.

Fortunately, there are plenty of resources to help. You can find online courses and software. Head over to **StartRightBook.com/resources** to see the resources I recommend. You can and should read everything you can get your hands on. This includes novels, nonfiction books, websites, newspapers, social media feeds, and anything else you can find in English.

Subscribe to YouTube channels and podcasts in English. Watch movies and TV shows in English. Ask friends if you are unsure of how to pronounce or express something correctly, and if you still do not understand, do not be afraid to ask for clarification.

Take note of any new vocabulary. Write the words down, then later look them up and truly understand what they mean and how they are correctly used. Then, you can incorporate them into your vocabulary more naturally.

Continue practicing and speaking with people every chance you get. You will be able to make marked improvements the more you practice. Don't forget about your written English—not just your papers but also your professional emails and the visual elements of any presentations you are preparing. A great way to get help with written English is by taking advantage of the university writing centre. Another tool you might want to use is Grammarly.com but do not depend on it or any software to catch everything.

For students heading to Quebec, you may want to invest similar time and effort into learning and practicing French. You will find it widely spoken in Montreal, Quebec City, Sherbrooke, and all across the province, as well as in many other places in Canada. In fact, you will meet people who speak only French. Do not forget it is one of the official languages of Canada, and the people of Quebec are very proud of their language and culture.

Learning French or English is extremely important. When I arrived, my IELTS score was sufficient to get into school, but I was not comfortable either speaking or writing. I would sometimes find myself in situations where I had to explain what I wanted by pointing and saying "this" or looking through a dictionary to find the right word. Keep working and you will keep improving.

Make Canadian Friends

Making friends is difficult for many people, no matter where they might be. When you are in Canada, as an international student, it can seem even harder. However, there are a few things that you can do to make the process a bit easier. One of the most important is to make sure you are willing to put yourself out there where you can find potential friends in the first place.

The famous author and businessman, Dr. Stephen R. Covey, offers this advice: *seek to understand and then to be understood*. Most people are looking to be heard and to get their point across, but they are not actually listening. They are just waiting for their turn to speak. People are not truly communicating when they do this. Learn to *listen* to what people are saying and to understand them before you respond.

You will find that most of the time, Canadians are thinking about the same sorts of things as people from other cultures. They might be thinking about their families, for example. Canadian students might have the same fears and worries that you have. We are all human, and we share similar fears and challenges.

Build Rapport with New Friends and Contacts

When you make new acquaintances and friends, try to build up a rapport with them. You can't begin any kind of relationship with another person until you've found a way to relate to them with respect. Seek to discover the things you share with the other person, and even if there's not much, developing a healthy understanding will reap long-term benefits.

It's important to remember that building rapport takes time. However, there is a saying: you only get one chance to make a first impression. The first time you meet someone, it is important to create a meaningful connection that starts to *establish* rapport.

Building rapport is a skill, and as with other skills, you can improve with practice. Here are some strategies for building rapport. At first, it may feel challenging to integrate and apply them, but with practice, you may be able to turn these strategies into habits that will stick with you in both your professional and personal life.

Find Common Ground

Identifying something that you have in common with another person can create an instant bond. Ask questions to learn more about him/her. If you're not sure where to start, look around you for clues. If you are meeting at a school club, for example, you already know you have a common interest. If they are wearing the jersey of a sports team you follow, or they are listening to music you like, those may also be interests you share.

Though it is tempting when you are in a new environment, you should never assume that people are similar to you just because they share your ethnic or religious background. To find true common ground and build rapport, start a conversation. You cannot just make assumptions. Be curious and attentive to details, and this will help you build relationships both now and in the future.

Be Yourself

"Be yourself; everyone else is already taken." – *Oscar Wilde*

One of the best ways to start building rapport is by being authentic. You can't pretend to have the same interest as someone else or make up a lie in order to talk to them and build rapport. Such fabrications will inevitably come to light, and the person will no longer trust you. When you speak to people, speak honestly. Avoid flattery or false interest. Give them sincere compliments.

Most people recognize when you are not being genuine, and they will not like it. Keep a positive attitude, smile, and make sure you are not tense. Meeting people is difficult and being nervous about it is natural. Try to be yourself, relax, and let your great qualities carry you through.

Be friendly but do not try too hard. Be alert to any behaviours that might make you come across as too needy. Such qualities will prevent you from building up a good rapport with the people you meet. Remember that rapport cannot be forced.

Choose Open-Ended Questions

When you meet someone new, try to ask questions that will garner a response that goes beyond a simple yes or no so you can open up greater possibilities for communication and dialogue. People often like to talk about the things that interest them, as well as about themselves and their ideas. Questions that begin with *why* or *how* can be an effective place to begin. Listen closely to their answers, and, in most cases, it is in those answers that you will find clues that will help you formulate your next open-ended question and keep the conversation going. By asking open-ended questions, you will get more engagement, and it will be possible to find common ground on which you can build rapport and your relationship.

Be Empathetic

You will also want to make sure you are as empathetic as possible with the people you are talking to. It's a huge aspect of building rapport. Learning how other people see the world and how things affect them can help give you a better perspective of them as a whole person. When you can empathize, it becomes much easier to build rapport.

Everyone Has Boundaries

You need to be mindful of boundaries when you are communicating, and you need to make sure you respect those boundaries. You do not want to get overly personal, asking too many questions, or probing into subjects that are clearly unprofessional and make people feel uneasy. If you happen to notice any body language that suggests they are uncomfortable, it is time to move onto another topic in the conversation, or, end the conversation altogether and allow the person to exit gracefully.

Cues – Verbal and Nonverbal

When you are trying to build up a rapport, it's not just what you say but also how you say it. The tone of voice you use, the volume, and even the pace at which you speak are all significant. Keep in mind that nonverbal cues, such as eye contact, gestures, and other body language are equally crucial.

Typically, you are going to want to smile. Shake hands—be firm but not forceful. Maintain eye contact without staring. Try to look the other person in the eyes around 60% of the time. Avoid distractions. The person you are with should be the focus of your attention—not your phone, your computer, or the screen on the wall showing the baseball game.

Try to maintain good posture and turn your body toward the other person. Do not cross your arms, as this can come across as being closed off. Strive to be welcoming and have a relaxed position and open body language. Speak clearly, don't rush your thoughts, and nod when appropriate.

Not long after I arrived in Canada, I gifted a bouquet of flowers to a Canadian girl as a sign of appreciation for her help with my school assignments. While back home, it is customary to give flowers to women on any suitable occasion irrespective of age, status or relationship, this girl interpreted my gesture as a sign of love and thought I was interested in dating her. This was certainly not my objective, and it resulted in a VERY awkward situation. It is easy to make assumptions since men and women from different cultures interact quite differently and it is easy to make a mistake. Research and understand local customs, watch for cues, and ask a friend if you are unsure.

Exercise: Break the Ice with Conversation Starters

If you get nervous talking with people, it can be helpful to prepare some icebreakers. If you happen to be taking the same courses or you are at the same meeting, that could be a great place to start. Of course, there are plenty of other topics that can also be used. For example, you might want to ask about their day or how they spent the weekend. Ask people what they do, where they are from, how they heard about the club or the concert, or anything else that makes sense at the moment. In Canada, the weather is often a great place to start.

The hardest part of starting conversations is speaking that first word. It is important to get over that fear or to at least get a good enough grasp of it that you don't let it dissuade you from making new friends. Remember that you can take breaks, especially if your personality tends to be on the quiet side.

For this exercise, brainstorm to come up with a few ideas for icebreakers. Remember to choose subjects that you are going to be comfortable talking about. Stay professional and authentic. Make a list of your best ideas.

Get a Buddy

You will find that having a friend or two will help make your transition much easier. Perhaps someone you met during orientation, or your roommate, or even someone that you met in the cafeteria will become your first friend. That person is very important, but don't limit yourself to just one friend.

Choose your friends wisely. Earlier I told the story about the friend who betrayed me and lied to her boyfriend about how I was flirting with her. Find good people who have similar interests and goals. Some international student associations on campus will set you up with a buddy to help with your transition. Make sure to inquire.

Manage Relationships Back Home

You probably want to keep in touch with your family back home. You may also have some old friends who you want to maintain contact with at least on a semi-regular basis. Fortunately, this tends to be easy. You can talk through social media, chat online, or make phone calls. You can also send post cards, and they may want to mail you packages of goods and treats from back home.

All of that is well and good. However, you want to make sure you are the one setting the timetable for when and how you will communicate with one another. Sometimes you need to focus on your priorities, for example, projects and exams, or you just need some mental space. They will not know this unless you make it clear. You should not feel guilty about setting your boundaries and, if you do not set them, there is a good chance that your parents and friends from home will not respect your independence and privacy as much as you might like. Set up a time every week or so that you plan to get in touch and base it on your needs.

It might feel a bit strange at first dictating to your parents and friends when you will be available to talk with them, but if you do not, they will still be controlling you from afar. Remember, you are here to gain independence, not just to lengthen your leash.

Manage Stress

All students get stressed. It doesn't matter where you are going to school, stress will find a way to affect you, and it will continue to get worse unless you do something about it. I have been through the stress of working hard to get good grades and depriving myself of sleep to study. I used to drink coffee to stay up and eventually that stopped working. I moved to caffeine pills, which were just as unhealthy. Then, I moved to energy drinks, and after that, on to harder things. These worked in the beginning, but then I had a big crash. This increased my stress even more. I became more tired, and I began to cram before exams. During this time, I was accused of plagiarism and had to defend myself, which increased the stress even more.

I do not want you to go through the same levels of stress that I and so many others have had to endure, so I will give you some quick, surefire tips on how to manage your stress.

- **Exercise:** Working out regularly is easily one of the best ways to reduce stress and relax. Exercise improves your body and your mood. You feel great after exercising. I enjoyed working out so much that I eventually went on to get certified as a personal trainer, which helped me earn some money when I was in school. Set fitness goals for yourself, just as you did with your other goals.
- **Relax the Muscles:** Your muscles get tense when you are stressed. You can keep them loose and reduce stress when you stretch, practice yoga, get a massage, or take a hot bath or shower.
- **Get Enough Sleep:** I know that getting sleep while at university is a struggle. However, if you want to keep your stress levels under control, it is something you will have to do. You follow a schedule for school, exercise, work, and free time, so why not add getting to bed at a decent hour onto that list?
- **Deep Breathing and Meditation:** Deep breathing and meditation are wonderful tools for relaxation. They can also help you focus. You can learn to meditate through books, apps, or even videos on YouTube. It is one of the easiest things you can do, but it is truly good for you.
- **Eat Well:** It is said that you are what you eat. While it might sound silly, it really is true. If you constantly eat foods that are bad for you, then you will not be as healthy as you could be. You will feel run down, and you will not have energy, which can add to your stress.

- **Stay Away from Nicotine, Alcohol, Caffeine, and Drugs:** Some caffeine in moderation might be okay, but you should never overdo it. Caffeine is addictive, as is nicotine and many drugs. Your best course of action for the sake of your health is to avoid them.
- **Talk About Your Problems:** Whether you see a therapist—and there are services on campus to help you find one—or you have some good friends who you can talk to about your problems, it really does help to talk out your issues.
- **Take a Break:** Working hard is great, but sometimes, you need to take a break and step away. When you feel this need, follow your intuition. It might be a good time to meditate or head to the gym. You will be more efficient when you get back to work.
- **Enjoy Your Hobbies:** What types of hobbies do you enjoy? Maybe you like reading or drawing. When you are feeling stressed, and even when you aren't, taking some time to engage in your hobbies will make you feel good. It will help push away stressful thoughts that might otherwise be creeping into your mind.
- **Go Easy on Yourself:** We are our own worst critics in most cases. We are very hard on ourselves when we make mistakes, compounding our stress. It's essential to learn how to forgive and go easier on yourself. Everyone makes mistakes. Learn from them but do not beat yourself up over them.

- **Identify Your Stressors and Find Ways to Eliminate Them:** What are the main things that cause stress in your life? If you have people in your life who are encouraging you to do something that is unhealthy or will interfere with your overall plans, maybe it is time to cut ties with those people. If you are stressed about a course you are taking, it might be time to double-down on your studying or talk with the advisor about finding a tutor. Take time to think about the issues causing your stress and find ways to limit or remove them from your life.
- **Start a Journal:** When in doubt or feeling anxious, start writing. It will bring clarity of thought.

No one lives a stress-free life. But there are solutions. As soon as you start to feel the weight of stress, use one or more of the above tips to help reduce it. They really do work.

What to Do If You Get Sick

Even if you take good care of yourself, there will come a time at school when you feel ill. You will get sick, even when you are eating right and exercising. Because there are so many people on campus, in classes, in the cafeteria, and in residence, colds and the flu tend to spread rather quickly. When you are feeling under the weather, listen to healthcare professionals. You should rest, hydrate, and eat healthy food. Vitamin C and sometimes chicken soup (or, a soup of your choice) can help you feel a bit better. In Canada, unlike in some other countries, you do not go to the hospital unless it is a serious medical emergency.

However, you might need to go to the doctor at some point. Universities typically have healthcare services on campus or nearby. While you are healthy, you should become familiar with the regulations that apply to international students who need access to the healthcare system. All international students in Canada are required to have health insurance. Coverage will vary from one province to another. In some provinces, students are covered by provincial health care plans. At some schools, student fees include health insurance. However, if you are in a province or at a school where you are not covered, then you must arrange for private health insurance coverage. Your school can assist you.

Exercise: Get Fit

Physical fitness is very important, not only for your health but also for the way you look and feel about yourself. So, for this exercise, we are going to be taking things literally.

Study the school website. Find a couple of ways that you will be able to get in some exercise on campus. Perhaps there are trails you can run or walk. Maybe there is a fitness centre with a pool or gym you can use. Consider joining a team or club on campus that organizes a sport you enjoy. If you cannot find what you like on campus, look off campus. Most Canadian cities are filled with public community centres and private gyms that offer many options for all budgets.

Commit to exercising at least three times per week and put the times in your calendar or diary.

Be Proactive

Because so many international students are nervous when they first arrive in Canada, they are *reactive*. They wait for things to happen before they respond. They do not get out there and make connections and friends. They are not looking for interesting clubs to join. It is as though they are trying to become invisible. If this is your attitude when you arrive, you are likely to have a more difficult time. At best, you will be seen as standoffish. Others might think you do not care or that you do not like them and do not want to learn about your new environment and culture.

Instead, you need to be proactive and take charge of your situation. You need to be the one willing to take more chances and talk with people you meet. You need to be proactive when it comes to taking care of your health and well-being, as well as when it comes to your studies.

Begin with the End in Mind

Remember those goals that you wrote down in the exercise in Chapter 3? You likely have a good idea about the type of career you want, and you might also be starting to develop strong ideas of what you want out of other aspects of your life. This is important, and it is good that you have been forward thinking. If you begin your journey as an international student in

Canada with goals in mind, you will find it easier to stick to your path.

The things you are doing now should propel you forward to the end that you want for yourself. If you have this mindset from the very beginning, you will not end up delaying the achievement of your goals. You can pattern your life around things that will help you reach those goals. Simple as that. Of course, I realize how complicated it can be to get into this mindset. You will have a lot going on when you arrive in Canada. You will have distractions and worries that you cannot get out of your head. Learn to focus on your goals and dreams. It gives you more direction when you are trying to decide what needs to be done.

Get to Know the Teachers/Professors

During your first 90 days, it is also essential to get to know your teachers, professors, and instructors better. They want you to succeed, and, similar to mentors, they will help keep you accountable. Being honest, doing your work, asking questions, and being engaged all go a long way toward helping with this. You might even want to volunteer in the classroom if you have time available. This allows them to see that you are willing to work, and that makes them more likely to become friendly with you.

In addition, you need to be respectful, and know how to communicate courteously with your professors. This includes email communication. Follow these simple "netiquette" rules:

- The subject headers should be descriptive and formal.
- The salutations at the start of the email should be professional, such as Dear Professor [Last Name], before adding the comma, hitting enter, and starting the email.
- Keep the email lean and to the point. You do not want to ramble or rant.
- Add some humanity to the email, such as mentioning something that was said in class or something that you believe the professor would want to know because it is in their field.
- Steer clear of using emojis and Internet lingo, such as LOL.
- Close out the email respectfully with your First and LAST NAME (Last name in caps) and student number.

Following a few of these simple rules will serve you well, both now, in your emails to professors, as well as in future, when emailing bosses and managers.

Get a Mentor

It cannot be stated enough just how important it is to have a mentor. This is true when you are first starting school, as well as throughout your career. A mentor at the university can help you navigate the system better.

I have had a mentor at every phase of my life: a principal at my high school, an international student advisor at university, successful businessmen and women as I was transitioning to the job market, and my first boss. My mentors would challenge me with new projects and provide much needed feedback. While a good mentor will act as a guide and a helping hand, they are not going to do the work for you.

Keep in mind that you are not just going to approach someone and tell them that you have decided to become their mentee. You first have to build a relationship and establish rapport with these individuals. Build mutual trust first. Once you have, it becomes easier to ask for help and mentorship.

As you start to meet more people, you will find some are going to be better suited to mentoring you. Identify three people and ask them to mentor you. Make sure to do your research about their background and communicate why being mentored specifically by them will help you.

If one of your chosen mentors says no, do not take it personally. People are busy and your chosen mentor may have too much to do already. Instead accept the no gracefully and move on to the next person on your list.

Model Behaviour

As you are trying to figure out who you are, you will find it helpful to identify someone you admire who can be a good role model. In certain cases, this might be someone you have considered as a mentor. It might also be one of your professors or student club leaders. It could be just about anyone who has the traits and the drive that you want to have as well. Model your behaviours after someone who has taken a path that is like the one you want to follow. Find an opportunity to engage with your role model on social media, via email, or by phone, and ask a question or two. They have already blazed the trail you are on.

Don't Take Bad Advice

Throughout your life, you are going to receive advice from a large number of people. Some will be friends and family. Some will be your mentors or teachers. Others might simply be people you randomly strike up a conversation with. Sometimes they will provide you with great advice.

Other times, they will have bad advice—even though they might believe they are doling out sage-like wisdom. When you get advice you know is bad, do not take it. Your intuition will tell you. Do not follow bad advice just because you want to make someone feel happy and appreciated. After all, bad advice is likely to hurt you and not them. Bad advice can be very expensive, financially and emotionally.

Many years ago, I received bad advice from an academic advisor. He told me I should neither pursue a specialization in international business nor go on exchange since I already was an international student. My intuition told me there was something wrong with this advice, and I listened to my intuition. I ended up specializing in international business and going on an exchange to Paris which was a highlight of my undergraduate degree. As a matter of fact, if I had taken his advice, I would not have started a career in international education since my first trip abroad as a recruiter took place during my exchange semester.

Get Good Grades

The whole point of going to a new school or university is to get an education. Naturally, you want to get good grades. However, with the excitement of moving to Canada and adapting to the new culture and language, you might be worried about whether you will be able to get and maintain good grades. Maybe you got good grades in your home country. You might be asking yourself whether the marking standards will be similar.

Fortunately, there are things you can do to ensure your grades are as good as possible.

Do you know the big rock experiment? Take a bucket and fill it half full of small pebbles. Then, try to fit several big rocks into the bucket, placing them on top of the pebbles. The problem is that they cannot all fit. Empty the bucket and start over. This time, put the big rocks in the bucket first, followed by the pebbles. Notice how the pebbles neatly fill in the spaces around the big rocks. This time everything fits! The difference is the order in which the rocks and pebbles were placed in the bucket. In this experiment, big rocks represent your most important things. Pebbles represent all the little everyday things that suck up your time, such as chores, texting, errands, and interruptions, etc. The moral of the story? If you don't take care of your big rocks first, they will not get done. Dr. Stephen R. Covey, the author of *The 7 Habits of Highly Effective People* said, "The key is not to prioritize what is on your schedule, but to schedule your priorities."

For me, getting good grades and completing major projects both inside and outside the class were priorities, and I proactively scheduled them in my calendar. This success habit allowed me to graduate with distinction, and along the way, enjoy numerous projects and hobbies.

I also discovered the power of Pareto's Principle (also known as the 80/20 rule). Roughly 80% of the effects arise from 20% of the causes. In simple terms, this means that 80% of my academic success came from 20% of the work and effort I put in. The key to successfully applying the Pareto Principle to academic work is making the most of the 20% of your time that will produce 80% of your results. There are a few ways to ensure maximum productivity when studying.

Be Productive

Always look for ways that you can be more productive. However, make sure you understand how to stay healthy while being productive. Earlier in the book, I talked about my dance with caffeine and other substances, and how these can be dangerous. You cannot work yourself to the bone and then expect coffee, nicotine, or other drugs to give you more energy. Instead, you need to find smarter and better ways of being more productive.

Technology has made many aspects of life easier, including studying. You might want to check out some of the productivity tools available today. There are many different types. Let's look at a few and at some popular examples.

- **Calendars:** These tools help you keep track of your schedule. Some popular options include Google Calendar and Outlook.
- **Notes:** Trello, Evernote, and Microsoft OneNote are popular options that will help you quickly and easily write notes you can access on any device that has the app. Evernote will allow you to save and organize articles, PDFs, video, sound, image, and more.
- **Distraction:** If you find that you are often distracted when you should be studying or writing, you might want to use a tool like Write Monkey. It will launch in full-screen mode and provide a distraction-free environment. You could try Heyfocus to block apps and distracting websites. Stayfocused is similar, but it is a browser extension.
- **File Storage and Sharing:** Google Drive and Dropbox are tools that will let you keep your study material and the items you are writing in a safe place. You will be able to access the material no matter where you are, as long as you have an Internet connection.

- **Task Managing:** There is a tool called Nirvana that will help record tasks, through email or the smartphone app, which can then be organized and tracked. You can even add contacts. Finished work can be exported to your computer.
- **Collaboration:** Slack and Basecamp are powerful online productivity tools for collaborating with other people. They can be great for class projects, study groups, and even friend groups.

These are some of the productivity tools you might find useful. Keep your eyes peeled for others. New ones come online all the time. Just make sure the tools themselves are not too distracting!

Stop Multitasking

At first glance, those who multitask might seem like they are very productive. However, when you take a closer look, you will often find this is not the case. They have a lot of work happening all at once, but very little is actually being accomplished. When the mind's attention is divided among all these different tasks, it becomes difficult to shift focus each time you turn to a different project. Ultimately, it will take longer to get the work done. If you had just focused on one thing at a time and given it 100% of your attention, you would have found that it went faster and that you had better results.

Develop a Study Ritual

It is important to develop a method of studying that works and to follow that method each time you study. People will naturally have different ways of studying, and you need to find what works for you. Since you have been in school for such a large part of your life, you probably already have a good idea of what study techniques work best for you. It's now time to adapt them to your new environment.

Some people like to listen to music while they are studying. It can help drown out other sounds that are distracting. If you do listen to music, try listening to something that does not have lyrics. They can be distracting. Classical music, soundtracks, and even the sound of the ocean can help you to concentrate. Some people feel that the only way they can study is in the library where it is completely silent. Maybe you need to have a cup of green tea each time you study.

Everyone has a ritual. Find what works for you and make it a habit.

Get into a routine, not only for studying, but also with other elements of your life. For example, having a good morning routine to follow now and even when you are finished school can help set up the day for success. Perhaps you like to get up, have a quick workout, a warm shower, and then eat breakfast. Find a morning routine that works for you.

I get up at 4 a.m., six times a week. I then meditate for 65 minutes, write in my journal, and exercise in the gym, pool, or outside. I have breakfast, drop off my kid at school, and start my workday by 9 a.m. This is my morning ritual which I tremendously enjoy.

Put Together a Study Group

Starting or joining a study group can be a huge benefit for a host of reasons. For starters, it means you will be able to go over the material with other people who are also taking the class. You can talk about what you are learning to get more insight into it. If you are going to be starting one of these groups, make sure you assemble a group that is serious about studying. Maybe you should "interview" candidates to make sure they are going to be able to add to the group rather than be a distraction.

This doesn't mean that you can't have an enjoyable time with the study group. You should be able to have fun, and it is perfectly natural that you will become friends. It is a great way to meet new people. Make sure everyone respects the time set aside for the study group. Socializing should be postponed until after the study session is over.

Be Engaged in Your Classes

Another way to get good grades is to make sure you are engaged in your classes. Sit near the front. Arrive earlier than everyone else and be the first to ask questions. Of course, make sure the questions you ask are pertinent. Be friendly to the professors and their teaching assistants and pay close attention during the lesson. When you walk into the classroom, keep negative and distracting thoughts outside. Enter with a positive attitude and be willing to focus on learning. When you combine engagement along with the other tips in this section, you will find that it can help keep your grades where they belong.

Exercise: What's Cool About You?

No matter how strong you are, no matter how much you evolve, there are going to be times when your self-confidence gets battered and bruised. If you want to reach your full potential, you need to protect your confidence. It's one of the most valuable things you have, and you need to nurture it. You need tools that can help you to regain your confidence. You will find that doing this exercise can be quite helpful whenever you feel like you have taken a hit.

When you are feeling down, think about what is cool about *you*. Sure, it might seem a little out there, but I promise this can really work, even though it might feel like a difficult question. It's important to ask. For this exercise, I want you to make a list of the top ten cool things about you.

When you have completed the list, you will see that even though you might have had some setbacks and hits to your self-confidence, you have a lot going on. You've done a lot. You're pretty cool. This exercise is a great boost when you need it. Try it out right now.

Visit **StartRightBook.com/resources** to access a worksheet for this exercise.

Chapter 10: The First Year in Canada

"Life isn't about finding yourself. Life is about creating yourself." – George Bernhard Shaw

Once you have the first 90 days out of the way, you might believe that all the worry and stress are behind you. Well, there's some good news and some bad news. First, the good news. You have proven that you have what it takes to persevere and succeed, and that's great. However, it's just the start of your journey. There is still a lot more work ahead. But that's okay. I believe in you. I know that you are determined to succeed.

What Habits Do You Need to Succeed in the First Year?

If you hope to succeed in your first year and beyond, make sure you are maintaining the good habits described in the last chapter. You should be exercising, so you can stay healthy and in shape. You should be eating right, and you should be getting plenty of sleep. You should have a study group that is working to help everyone improve their grades. You should be integrating well. However, as time passes, there are some other things that you will want to do and habits you will want to adopt.

Be Solution Oriented

Regardless of what I am doing in life, I have found that being solution oriented is the best way to tackle any problem. Instead of lamenting that something is going to be difficult, I try to find solutions. This makes handling even the biggest problems seem much more feasible. Let me give you an example.

The first time I met my wife Yuliya, we were in middle school. We met briefly, but we were from the same city. I later went to Canada, as you know, and she went to Moscow. Both of us were international students. However, we were extremely far apart. During one of our summer breaks, when we were both back home, we met again and fell in love. We realized there was a significant distance between us. Nonetheless, instead of giving up, we started a long-distance relationship.

Naturally, I wanted to see her more. Instead of just being sad that I could not, I started to look for solutions. I had studied marketing and business in school, and when I graduated, I had two job options available. I could work for a pharmaceutical company in Toronto, which would require me to move from Vancouver, or I could work at the high school where I had studied and be a marketer/recruiter for them. I chose to educate people because it felt better.

However, the career as a recruiter would also allow me to travel and potentially see Yuliya more often. I figured I would apply myself to learning how to become a travel hacker. I studied frequent flyer programs, and miles and points that I could earn on my credit card. What I learned allowed Yuliya and I to travel when we had free time. In the first three years of our relationship, we saw much of the world and went to many places in Europe, as well as to the Maldives, Morocco, Japan, and more. After we married, we even took three honeymoons!

I was able to find a great solution to a problem that other people might have let get the better of them. I know you can do this as well. You can square off against the problems you are facing and find a way to deal with them.

Exercise: Stay Happy

Are you happy? A happy person tends to be healthier and has less stress. A happy person is often more productive as well. However, for many people, it is hard to stay happy. Most people have moments of happiness, but they are often fleeting. You might be *satisfied* with where you are and the things you are doing. But you might not be truly happy. It is important that you find ways that you can stay in the "happy zone" as much as possible. You will feel better emotionally, psychologically, and physically when you do.

So, ask yourself what actually makes you happy. Often, it is to love and be loved. Many people love helping others as well. However, it does not always have to be something as grand as love that makes you happy. In fact, what makes people happy typically differs from one person to another. Sure, we have a lot in common when it comes to the things that make us happy, but there are plenty of differences as well.

Examine yourself and who *you* are, and then write down a list of the times that you have been truly happy or of the things that you know make you happy. It might be playing music. It might be a favourite TV show or movie that brings back some great memories. Maybe it is a hobby you enjoy.

Make a list of the things that make you happy and then commit to enjoying some of those things on a regular basis. This can help you stay happy no matter where you might be and what you might be facing.

Keep adding to that list as you find other things that you enjoy. This will ensure you have plenty of diversions for the times when you might be feeling a little down.

Improve Your Leadership Skills

If you haven't already joined a club, join one now and try to take on a leadership role. Keep in mind that leadership styles will differ from one country to another. You will need to learn who to work with and get a better understanding of the leadership style that works for you and the team you are leading. Simply by starting to work with others, you will be getting valuable experience and your leadership skills will grow. It's best to start your journey as a leader as early as possible in your schooling. The skills you learn will serve you well in the future.

As with other skills, you will get better the more that you practice. I applied for the UBC International Leader of Tomorrow Scholarship, but ultimately, I did not get it. Rather than quitting, I chose to prove that I was a leader by getting more involved in student life. I became the President of the International Student Association and was able to convince the university to establish a scholarship and offer better services to the students. My involvement with this club lead to more leadership roles and opportunities. I eventually received two prestigious community service and leadership awards. My experience proves that practice and perseverance can pay off, and I know you can find the same type of success in your own life.

Say Yes, Figure Out the Rest, and Don't Take No for an Answer

When an opportunity lands in your lap, it is important to grab it and appreciate the chance you have been given. Say yes, even if you are not quite sure how to proceed. You can learn as you go. For example, I was offered the chance to run a student organization, and I said yes without even thinking about it. Of course, I quickly realized that there was a lot of politics involved. The current president already had a successor in mind—and it was not me.

Still, I accepted the challenge even though there were no team members from the previous year, and there were no continuity documents. I persevered. I found a new mentor and built a new team.

One of my responsibilities was to raise sponsorship money and I had to do a lot of cold calling and emailing. Many people I reached out to said *no*, but I did not stop. Every time I heard *no*, I asked for a referral to someone else who might be able to help. By not taking *no* for an answer, I was able to secure sponsorship from two large corporations, both of which I found through referral. By saying *yes* and not taking *no* for the final answer, I was able to hone my leadership skills in a real-world environment.

Exercise: Do Anywhere Gratitude

Gratitude has been proven to make people happier and healthier. While you might not be able to force yourself to feel grateful, you can start to change the way you think. This "Do Anywhere" exercise is simple but very effective. All you need to do is think about five things in your life that you are truly grateful for. They can be large or small. It does not matter. The only thing that matters is that you are grateful for them.

Do this regularly and try to name a few different things each time. Before long, you will start to see there are many things in your life for which you can be truly grateful.

Visit **StartRightBook.com/resources** to access a worksheet for this exercise.

Manage Your Finances

When you are in school and after you have graduated, take good care of your finances. Proper financial management is essential in today's world and missteps can cause some serious problems for your credit and your well-being. To help you avoid these common mistakes, here are a few simple but effective tips.

One of the first things you need is a budget. You know how much money you have and how much you are able to bring in each month to pay for your living expenses. You need to establish your living expenses as well. How much do you spend on the essentials each month? How much are you able to save?

Develop a budget that ensures you are not overspending, as this is one of the ways that many people get into financial trouble. Learn to live within your means. You should not go out and party when you only have $20 left in your bank account. There are many tools and resources to make the process easier. Budgeting apps can track expenditures, save receipts, and more. Visit **StartRightBook.com/resources** to access recommended resources.

Putting some money into an emergency fund will help ensure you have a bit of cushioning in case you find yourself in financial trouble. For example, if you are working a part-time job that suddenly ends for one reason or another, it will be nice to have that extra money until you find your next job. This is something you should do throughout your life, not just when you are in school.

Build Your Personal Brand

"Start by knowing what you want and who you are, build credibility around it and deliver it online in a compelling way." – Krista Neher

Your personal brand is your reputation. When you interact with others, you are giving them an impression or a glimpse into the type of person you are. You have the opportunity to provide them with a good, memorable experience. However, you need to be consistent in the way you deliver these experiences in order to build a solid and cohesive brand. The brand will be what people think of you, and what they tell other people about you.

When you are building your personal brand, you need to focus on your strengths and your individuality, while making the choice to provide better interactions between you and those who you meet. This will create more opportunities for you later. Develop your personal brand both online and offline.

It is very important to start building your personal brand as soon as possible. Let me tell you why by sharing an experience. The infamous movie *Borat: Cultural Learnings of America for Make Benefit Glorious Nation of Kazakhstan* starring Sacha Baron Cohen came out the year I entered university. As I was the first student from Kazakhstan and probably the most famous one at my university, everybody started calling me Borat instead of Boris whether I was around or not. It did not take much time before everyone, even professors, was using this new name when talking to or about me. While some people thought that this was just a harmless nickname meant affectionately, I did get upset as it was paining me, my family, and my community in the inaccurate way Kazakhstan was depicted in a documentary-like movie. At that point I decided that I had to build a personal brand otherwise I would be stuck with my new nickname forever.

If you think that branding and personal marketing is something you do not need, you are sorely mistaken. To get a better idea of just how long branding has been around, and just how powerful it can be, let's look at what is alleged to have been the first resume in the world. It was written by Leonardo da Vinci when he was 30 years old and sent to the Duke of Milan, Ludovico il Moro. This is a translation.

> Most Illustrious Lord, Having now sufficiently considered the specimens of all those who proclaim themselves skilled contrivers of instruments of war, and that the invention and operation of the said instruments are nothing different from those in common use: I shall endeavor, without prejudice to anyone else, to explain myself to your Excellency, showing your Lordship my secret, and then offering them to your best pleasure and approbation to work with effect at opportune moments on all those things which, in part, shall be briefly noted below.

1. I have a sort of extremely light and strong bridges, adapted to be most easily carried, and with them, you may pursue, and at any time flee from the enemy; and others, secure and indestructible by fire and battle, easy and convenient to lift and place. Also methods of burning and destroying those of the enemy.

2. I know how, when a place is besieged, to take the water out of the trenches, and make endless variety of bridges, and covered ways and ladders, and other machines pertaining to such expeditions.

3. If, by reason of the height of the banks, or the strength of the place and its position, it is impossible, when besieging a place, to avail oneself of the plan of bombardment, I have methods for destroying every rock or other fortress, even if it were founded on a rock, etc.

4. Again, I have kinds of mortars; most convenient and easy to carry; and with these I can fling small stones almost resembling a storm; and with the smoke of these cause great terror to the enemy, to his great detriment and confusion.

5. And if the fight should be at sea, I have kinds of many machines most efficient for offense and defense; and vessels which will resist the attack of the largest guns and powder and fumes.

6. I have means by secret and tortuous mines and ways, made without noise, to reach a designated spot, even if it were needed to pass under a trench or a river.

7. I will make covered chariots, safe and unattackable, which, entering among the enemy with their artillery, there is no body of men so great but they would break them. And behind these, infantry could follow quite unhurt and without any hindrance.

8. In case of need, I will make big guns, mortars, and light ordnance of fine and useful forms, out of the common type.

9. Where the operation of bombardment might fail, I would contrive catapults, mangonels, trabocchi, and other machines of marvelous efficacy and not in common use. And in short, according to the variety of cases, I can contrive various and endless means of offense and defense.

10. In times of peace I believe I can give perfect satisfaction and to the equal of any other in architecture and the composition of buildings public and private; and in guiding water from one place to another.

11. I can carry out sculpture in marble, bronze, or clay, and also, I can do in painting whatever may be done, as well as any other, be he who he may.

> Again, the bronze horse may be taken in hand, which is to be to the immortal glory and eternal honor of the prince your father of happy memory, and of the illustrious house of Sforza.
>
> And if any of the above-named things seem to anyone to be impossible or not feasible, I am most ready to make the experiment in your park, or in whatever place may please your Excellency—to whom I comment myself with the utmost humility, etc.

Even though you might not be da Vinci, you have your own set of skills and great qualities that you bring to the table. When you are developing your personal brand, it's important to highlight them, whether it is in a resume, online, or in person.

For additional guidance about creating your personal brand, head over to **StartRightBook.com/resources.**

Exercise: Personal Brand for Career Success

Students who have strong personal brands are more likely to launch themselves into a successful career. Improving your personal branding is similar to preparing for a job interview, months in advance. Building your personal brand forces you to think about what you want out of life—and that is incredibly valuable.

Establishing a professional presence with a clear and concise image, reputation, and status is a must.

Personal marketing has never been more important, and your personal brand should communicate the best you have to offer.

Have you ever searched your name online? Search using your browser in incognito mode and look at the results. Are there any videos, photos, and news? If you see something inappropriate, update the privacy settings on your social media. You may have to untag yourself from photos your friends have posted.

Once, I found an inappropriate photo posted of me holding a bottle of Grey Goose vodka as a trophy after winning second place in the Vancouver Top Promoter competition. It did not convey an image of myself that I wanted to promote. I had to chase the web developer for months to get this photo removed from the Internet.

A great way to start to build your personal brand is to create a profile on LinkedIn. It is the best platform to showcase your credentials. The best time to start is now. Build your connections over time. Slowly but steadily add your friends, classmates, professors, advisors, prospective employers, etc. Over the years, I have been offered jobs, contracts, and partnerships through LinkedIn. This was because I consistently posted valuable information that was relevant to my network.

Here are the steps I am challenging you to take with this exercise:

First, sign up for LinkedIn, if you have not done so already. Build your online profile stating that you are a student and naming your college or university. Make sure to include some of your past work experience and achievements. This should take you no more than 30 minutes.

Second, start adding your professional connections such as professors, university staff you have interacted with, successful alumni you have connected with, and so on. Remember to add a short personal note that explains why you want to link with that person. Perhaps you have met at an event or you are inspired by their profile. Don't worry about the traditional resume until you have a specific job in mind. When you apply, your resume will have to be tailored, anyways.

Third, find the contact details of a career counsellor at your institution and send a request for a meeting within the next five days. You need to start tapping into career resources today or it will be too late. I know hundreds of students who come to me for advice on finding a part-time job or summer internship but are too late to the game. Do not be one of them. Take your career destiny into your hands. Career counsellors and coaches are super nice and helpful people, and they are there to help you figure out how to navigate a career during and after your studies.

If you want to take this to the next level, create a personal website (e.g., www.FirstNameLastName.com) and email (contact@FirstNameLastName.com), especially if you are a writer, artist, designer, etc. This is a great place to showcase your work for prospective employers and clients.

Chapter 11: Transitioning to the Job Market

"Of all the questions I have asked my readers this is the most important: What would you do if you weren't afraid? When you finally give wings to that answer then you have found your life's purpose." —Shannon L. Alder

Now, we are going to look even further into your future. As you head into your second, third, and fourth year studying in Canada, ask yourself what you want. You might be considering the same path I took. I knew that I was going to stay in Canada. I knew that I wanted to work in the same country where I had spent years getting my education. I also knew that this would not be easy. I had to think about exactly what I needed to do in order to make this happen.

Keep Building Your Network

Networking requires taking your rapport-building skills and using them to meet new people. International students are at a disadvantage in the beginning because they know few people or, as it was in my case, no one in Canada. Start building your network as soon as possible.

Ideally, you will start to network before you even arrive at the school. Emailing professors using the tips mentioned earlier, contacting school representatives such as recruiters and admissions officers, etc. can get you started before you land in Canada. However, you also need to keep adding to your network once you are in school.

As a student, you will find that you can actually leverage your network to your advantage. Invite alumni to coffee chats, for example. Not only will you learn more about them, but you can also ask them for a referral or introduction to someone else.

While you might not realize it, your network is really your net worth. A lot of success will depend on the people you know.

Sign up for networking events if you can find them in your area. They can be a great way to start meeting more people, including those that you never would have been able to meet otherwise. Then, come up with an *elevator pitch*. This is a short introduction that encapsulates who you are and what you offer. It is something that should be easy to develop if you have been working on your personal branding. Why is it called an elevator pitch? Imagine getting onto an elevator with someone who runs a company you've always wanted to work for. You want to tell your story to capture his or her attention and make an ask for whatever you are looking to accomplish. But time is limited. That person is going to get off the elevator. You might have only 15 seconds. So, you'd better be prepared. Make your pitch clear and compelling.

Building a great network will take a lot of time and energy, but it will be well worth it. It can be quite a bit of fun to meet all these new and interesting people.

Remember, that 80% of jobs are found through networking. Online job postings receive hundreds and sometimes thousands of applications, and, as an international student, your chances of being shortlisted for an interview are lower than your chances of getting in front of a prospective employer in person or on the phone by using your network. I personally have never landed a job when applying for an online posting. Every job I've ever been offered has been either through a referral or persistent networking. I got my job at Schulich by calling the hiring manager and telling her that I was in Toronto for two days and that I wanted to chat with her about a role I was really interested in (at that time, I lived in Vancouver). I ultimately got the job.

Get some business cards printed with your name, photo, phone, and email. Carry these around at all times. There are numerous occasions when these cards will help you stand out from the crowd at student networking events. Giving your card to someone with confidence shows your character and professionalism. Remember to shake hands firmly when you introduce yourself, but do not squeeze your new acquaintance's hands.

Get a Part-Time Job

When you are in school, whether you are at home or in Canada, it's important to pay attention to your studies. However, getting a part-time job can provide you with some nice benefits. Most students struggle with paying not only for their schooling, but also for everyday items such as food, as well as for the cost of going out and having a meal or seeing a movie once in awhile so they can enjoy life. Having a part-time job will provide you with additional funds.

You will also get a good lesson in money management. Because a part-time job is not going to make you wealthy, you will learn how to budget better. This knowledge, although it might not seem important right now, can be quite helpful in future. In fact, I suggest taking some of the money that you earn and stashing it away. You can reduce stress knowing there is somewhere to turn if an unexpected need arises. See the earlier section on creating an emergency fund.

There is, of course, also the benefit of being able to get actual experience, meet new people, and establish new contacts through your job. Whether you are working part-time at the front desk of a hotel, as a barista in a coffee shop, or anywhere else, you will gain experiences that are going to add to your education at the university and in life. You will learn how to deal with people, including customers and managers, who may not always have your best interests in mind. Becoming skilled at navigating these pathways will serve you very well.

It can also remind you that you want to do well in school, so you can pursue a career path and not have to rely on low-paying, unskilled jobs for the rest of your life. You might even be fortunate enough to get a part-time job in a field that already interests you, which could one day lead to a full-time job, allowing you to follow your dreams.

As an international student, it can be difficult to know exactly *how* to get a part-time job. I know that it is a struggle for many, and I've had my own share of disappointments. For example, I was extremely interested in fitness, and I wanted to work at Gold's Gym on campus part-time. However, because I didn't have experience, they would not hire me. That did not stop me, though, because I really wanted that job. So, I became educated on fitness, I developed my soft skills, and then, one day I introduced myself to the gym owner in the change room. It took longer to land that job, but I was more prepared when I finally did.

I also got a part-time job at the university's Career Centre. That job gave me valuable experience and money, as well as a deeper understanding of the business of education. It allowed me to start developing my online portfolio. Remember to always be learning and improving, even outside your studies. This will give you more skills and knowledge and help you get the job you want.

When you apply for part-time jobs, there will be times you are rejected and times that they never even contact you to let you know you did not get the job. This can be disheartening, but do not give up. It happens to everyone. Let's look at a few tips that might help increase your chances of landing a job.

If you cannot find something on campus, look off campus. Nearby places or those that are within a short drive if you have a car or use public transportation are great places to start. You can find job options online or use your network.

Put out as many applications as you can, and even look for online freelance work. Don't restrict yourself to one particular field. Check the university to see if they have any placement programs. Most of the time, these jobs are not simply going to land in your lap. You have to get out there and look for them.

Keep in mind that if there is interest in hiring you at any place where you apply, you will still need to undergo an interview. Dress appropriately, be respectful, and act confidently during the interview. Leave a good impression. Even if they do not offer you the job, you do not know how it might help you in the future. And if you are not the selected candidate, remember it is not the end of the world. There will be other opportunities.

If you are successful with landing an interview but you do not get the job, consider whether there is something you can learn from what happened in the interview. I encourage you to follow up with a call or email to the hiring manager to politely ask for feedback about why you were not successful. Maybe you did not have enough experience. If that is the case, find ways to get more experience, even if it means volunteering for a while or getting an internship. This will provide you with experience you can use on your resume and on job applications going forward. Use whatever feedback you receive from the hiring manager to make the changes that will give you a better chance at success the next time.

Get a Summer Internship

Getting a summer internship in Canada is a fantastic idea that can pay great dividends down the line. You will get a substantial amount of great experience with your internship. You will see what it is like to work in the real world, and maybe even in a field that interests you.

When it comes to finding an internship, there are a number of sources you can use. Start with your school. You have contacts in the form of friends, professors, people in your study group, etc., who might know about internships in your field. Ideally, they would be able to provide you with a recommendation, giving you a foot in the door. Also use Career Centre resources and your networking skills.

Having an internship will provide you with even more contacts and friends that you can rely on once you are through school. These contacts can help you later in life, and maybe you will even be able to help them out in a few years.

Interview for a Job

Interviewing for a job can be nerve-wracking for many people. However, think about all the things you have already done. You have picked up and moved to another country for a great education. You went without family or friends and you made it on your own. You will not let an interview stand in your way of living the life that you have always wanted. Compared to all you have already accomplished, the interview will be easy. Here are some additional tips to help you out.

- **Research the Company:** Take some time to learn about the company and who is in charge. Learn about the competitors, the competitive advantages the company has, etc. This shows you have done your homework, and you will be ready if they ask any questions about their company. Glassdoor.ca is a great place to learn about what current and former employees have to say about any given company, its leadership, compensation, etc.
- **Dress to Impress:** While you do not need to have a $3,000 suit, you still want to dress in appropriate clothing. There are some high-quality suits for sale in consignment and second-hand stores if your budget is small.
- **Be Friendly and Smile:** Just as you did when you were building rapport with people who became your friends and contacts, you will want to smile and be friendly with the interviewer. Never exhibit a standoffish or aggressive attitude when you begin an interview. Open and close on a positive note. Show confidence and remember to smile whether it is an in-person, video conferencing, or phone interview. That's right; even though

they might not be able to see your face, your smile will actually come through in the way you are delivering your words.
- **Know Your Selling Points:** Make sure you know and can articulate what your best points are and why you are right for the job. It's a good idea to have between three and five of these selling points prepared, so you can tell the interviewer why you want the job and why it should be yours.
- **Anticipate the Interviewer's Concerns:** Interviewers often need to look for ways to screen people out of the hiring process simply because there are so many candidates. Put yourself in their shoes and think of reasons they might not want to hire you. Then, create counterarguments as to why you are still the best person for the job.
- **Have Your Own Questions:** You do not want to work for a company without knowing more about them. Do some research. Prepare a few questions to ask during the interview.
- **Do Not Bring Up Salary or Wages at the Early Stages of the Process:** Wait until the recruiter or the hiring manager asks about your salary expectations or makes an offer. If you are asked about your expectations, politely state that you can work with the manager to find a number that is fair. Do not disclose your current salary, and, if they press, politely state that you are not comfortable discussing it at that moment.

Come prepared, throw out one or two facts that you learned about the person or company to strengthen the relationship, and do not be afraid to point out areas for improvement. For example, in an interview with one company, I waited for the right time and then pointed out that I had found several broken links on the website during my research. This demonstrated my genuine interest in the company and attention to detail.

During the interview, identify something you can follow up with in the days ahead. Surely, you will send a follow-up email within 24 hours, but offer to share something such as an article or a video. Just make sure it is relevant.

Negotiate Your Salary

Unlike in many countries, it is not very common in Canada to negotiate in day-to-day life. You do not go to a supermarket and negotiate with a cashier on the price of bananas. Whether you take one or 10, you pay a fixed price based on weight. However, it's often a different story when it comes to your salary.

The best strategy for effective salary negotiations requires research and preparation. You most certainly want to know the minimum wage, as well as employment standards, in the province where you work and live. As I write this book, the minimum hourly wage varies between $12 and $15. There is also a minimum of 10 days of vacation per year or 4% vacation pay on top of your salary if you are paid hourly. For full-time permanent jobs, you can find salaries on Glassdoor.ca and for positions in publicly funded organizations, such as universities, salary bands are published, and you can negotiate within the stated range.

Remember while you are researching to consider the overall compensation not just the base salary. Keep in mind that companies differ more and more when it comes to the benefits they provide their employees. You should ask about insurance and retirement plans. Are there vacations and learning funds available? Are there annual performance bonuses? Find out everything the company is able to offer.

In most cases, the negotiation process will begin when the prospective employer makes you an offer. Compare the offer to what you learned from your research. Make sure it will meet your needs and that it is in line with what someone with your level of experience and education would customarily receive. Remember to weigh in the benefits and what they could mean to you and your family. Make sure you are happy with the offer. Do not sell yourself short.

Understand that the person across from you at the negotiation table does not care what you want. They are thinking about how much value you will bring to the company. They care about their own face and evaluating how much liability you could be. In their mind they are asking, "What is in it for me?"

If, after all your deliberations, you're not happy with the offer, make a counteroffer. Be specific. Give reasons for why you think your counteroffer is more appropriate. If you have had or are having interviews with other companies, you could have some leverage when it comes to negotiating salary.

I've found that one of the best strategies in negotiations is to have a competing offer. I was able to use this strategy when negotiating one job contract. A prospective employer had made an offer, but it wasn't competitive. Fortunately, I had an offer from another company. I informed the hiring manager about it. I explained, however, that we were close and asked to work together towards a fair number. The decision-making process was expedited. I ended up signing an offer which was 40% higher than my salary at that time.

At the end of your negotiation process, you will either decline or accept what you've been offered. If you decide to accept despite being unhappy about the salary, you could ask for a salary review in a few months. Explain that even though you understand the company is not prepared to offer your desired salary now, you would like to re-negotiate after you've had, for example, six months to demonstrate your performance.

Sometimes, if you are just starting out in the field, you might have to take the entry level salary and position yourself to re-negotiate your salary in 3 to 12 months time. Just make sure your offer is fair.

Practice your negotiation skills with a friend, mentor, or advisor in a Career Centre. Practice is the key for effective salary negotiation.

In his book, *I Will Teach You To Be Rich,* and on his website, Ramit Sethi provides many valuable tips on salary negotiation and things you should avoid.

- **Not negotiating at all.** Some people are afraid of the negotiation table. They worry that they aren't good at interviews or that there's no point. Getting a higher salary is always worth the risk.
- **Telling the people interviewing you your current or previous salary.** This will destroy your ability to make a substantial leap forward because they will already know what you were making before. They will keep their offer as low as possible, while keeping it tempting. Keep your salary private.
- **Not planning ahead.** You need to be ready for the negotiation. Be ready to justify what you are asking for. Know what you are worth to them and how to express it.
- **Turning down offers too soon and burning bridges.** If you decide to turn down a job offer, don't burn bridges. You never know where the person sitting on the other side of the table will be in three years.
- **Giving up too soon.** If you give up too quickly, you aren't negotiating. You are simply taking what they say you are worth. Make it a point to actually negotiate. You might not get everything you want, but negotiation is a game of give and take.

File Taxes

All individuals in Canada who earn an income, no matter its source, should file their personal tax return. It is required by law. Fortunately, it tends to be relatively easy to file your taxes. You will need to make sure they are filed by a set deadline which is generally April 30 each year unless you are self-employed. Your employer and school will provide the information slips that you will need in order to complete the forms.

You have the option of filing your taxes electronically using software or in hard copy by filling out paper forms. Of course, you can pay someone to take care of filing your taxes, but I recommend figuring out how to do it on your own, especially when your financial situation is not complicated.

There are tax clinics available at universities and colleges. The first time I filed my taxes, I was surprised to receive a $150 refund even though I did not earn any income that year. Filing taxes rarely pays you, but it did for me that first time.

When you fill out your tax return, you will need to report your income, which is any money earned through employment, investments, and self-employment, as well as the benefits you receive from government. Then, you will claim your deductions, tax credits, and expenses. You need to keep all your tax documents for at least six years in case the government decides to audit your account. You should also keep receipts for anything you are planning to deduct.

There is plenty of information online, including guides at the Canada Revenue Agency website, and many of the software programs will walk you through what you need to do.

Get Micro-Credentials

I found it beneficial when I was an international student to earn micro-credentials. For example, I became certified as a personal trainer because I was interested in fitness and wanted to work at a gym. By getting this credential, I was able to make more contacts and find other avenues of employment. You can and should do the same.

I was also certified in Salesforce, Google Analytics, and Hootsuite. These have helped me in my life and career. But there are many other micro-credentials available. Getting micro-credentials like this will not only provide you with more job opportunities—you might also find a new career path you really love.

To learn more about micro-credentials I recommend, go to **StartRightBook.com/resources**.

What's the Difference Between a Job, a Career, and a Life Mission?

You might be under the impression that all these terms are interchangeable. However, that's not the case. If you are fortunate enough to have a career or job that aligns with your life mission, then they *could be*, and you are lucky. However, most of the time, there is quite a bit of a difference between them. Let's take a closer look.

A job is a three-letter word that some people jokingly say means "Just Over Broke." It's something that you do to make money and make ends meet. But it is not something that you necessarily went to school for, and it is not likely something about which you are passionate.

A career is something that offers growth. It might be something that you are interested in or good at. The career might pay more than a "job", and it might have more benefits. Ultimately, it is all about what the career can do for you. Does it offer you a comfortable lifestyle? While that's great from a financial perspective, your career still might not be your life mission.

What is a life mission? It's a way you will contribute to society. There is a saying I heard from a friend of one of my professors: "It is a luxury to pursue what makes you happy, but it is a moral obligation to pursue what you find meaningful." Another saying you might have heard and that really applies to your life mission is this: "The two most important days in your life are the day you are born and the day you find out why." Your life mission is something that is bigger than just a career. Furthermore, it will be unique for everyone.

Exercise: Personal Reflection and Introspection Essay

An important aspect of your life after graduation will be your career. Selecting the right career to fit your personality and your ambitions is critical to your future happiness and success. Thinking through what this could be for you prior to entering the workforce will serve you well. This exercise is intended to help you begin and/or continue this important introspective exercise. By no means is it comprehensive, but it could help you now and for many years into the future.

Write a five- to ten-page essay that considers your ideal career in three time horizons: after graduation, five years from that date, and twenty years from that date. When completing this essay, please do not discuss your industry, job function, or role. Discuss only what your surroundings look like (e.g., the décor, colour of the walls, office/cubicle/other), the specifics of what you do (e.g., meetings, phone calls, travelling, thinking, writing), your general thoughts or feelings as you move throughout the day, what people are doing or saying around you, your aspirations, stresses, joys, etc. In other words, in as much detail as possible, visually capture your ideal day-to-day work environment for each time period.

This exercise was by far the most informative activity of my undergraduate studies and helped me shape my career choices.

Chapter 12: Transitioning to Permanent Residency

"We are citizens of the world. The tragedy of our times is that we do not know this."– Woodrow Wilson

If you are interested in becoming a permanent resident or citizen of Canada, you should be aware of the requirements and the process involved. In this chapter, I will be going over the basics. Check out Canada's website on immigration, refugees, and citizenship, which features a wealth of information.

Who is Eligible?

To become a Canadian citizen, you will need to first become a permanent resident. As of the writing of this book, to become a permanent resident, you will need to qualify under either the Canadian Experience Class or one of the Provincial Nominee programs. These programs are tied to your education and employment in Canada. The requirements can change at any moment, so make sure to consult the official website.

As a permanent resident, you can qualify for domestic tuition, receive social benefits such as health care coverage, live, work, or study anywhere in Canada, apply for Canadian citizenship, and get protection under Canadian law and the Canadian Charter of Rights and Freedoms. You are not allowed to vote or run for political office, or to hold certain jobs that need high-level security clearance.

Currently, to become a citizen, you need to have lived in Canada for three of the last five years and filed taxes if required under your particular circumstances, and then you will have to pass a test on your rights and responsibilities and your knowledge of Canada. You also need to prove your language skills. Let me remind you again that these requirements can change. Always check the official website.

It is important to note that you do not automatically become a Canadian citizen after marrying a Canadian. The spouse of a citizen of Canada will still have to meet the above requirements. In addition, note that a permanent resident is someone who is a citizen of another country, but who has been given permanent resident status by immigrating to Canada. Students and foreign workers are not permanent residents. You must apply to become a permanent resident, and only after gaining this status can you move forward with your goal of citizenship.

Exercise: Study for Citizenship

In order to become a Canadian citizen, most permanent residents will need to take a Canadian citizenship test. The questions cover a range of different topics including history, geography, economy, laws, symbols, and the government. There are 20 questions, and you will be given half an hour to complete the test. The answers are either multiple choice or true or false. You can choose to take the test in either English or French. Applicants for citizenship must answer at least 15 (75%) questions correctly to pass the test.

The questions for the citizenship test are based on *Discover Canada*, the official citizenship study guide which can be downloaded for free online. It is a great way to learn about the country either before arriving or at any point during your time in Canada. While most feel that the test will not be a problem, some get nervous because the stakes are high. Therefore, you should take the time now and read through the study guide. Practice the test online and make sure you aren't just trying to memorize answers. Make sure you truly understand the material.

Chapter 13: Success Habits for a Lifetime

"Your time is limited, so don't waste it living someone else's life."– Steve Jobs

Whether you are just thinking about moving to Canada for your schooling or you are already in the country and starting your new life, it is important that you stay balanced. There are a number of ways you can do this, some of which we've covered in the book already. You know that you need to have a balance between your studies, social life, and work. You know that you need to make time to exercise, so you can stay fit and healthy.

Exercise: Stay in Balance

An exercise that you might want to do regularly is The Balance Wheel, which you can find at **StartRightBook.com/resources**. There are eight sections on the wheel. These include:

- Study/Work
- Health/Sport/Wellness
- Relationships

- Personal Growth
- Environment/Community Living
- Finance/Money
- Hobby/Energy
- Spirituality/Belief/Purpose

You begin by assigning a "score" to each segment of the wheel based on how satisfied you are with that aspect of your life. Score them from 0 to 10, and then on each segment, fill in or draw a line to indicate the level of your score. If you are in balance, the image will still look like a wheel at the end. If not, you will easily be able to see where things are out of balance, and the areas you need to work on to get back on track. If you can, work with a friend or coach to complete this exercise.

Exercise: Gain Clarity

It might take some time before you really understand exactly what your life mission is, and that's okay. However, I believe that it's important to start thinking about this as early as possible. Your life mission and your personality, *who you are*, help to inform one another. The best time to start thinking about this is right now.

Though it may feel ephemeral when you first start to think about it, allow it enough time to take shape. As you learn more about who you are and what you want to do for society, you will be able to further refine your ideas.

You can use the Clarity Tool at **StartRightBook.com/resources** to help determine your life mission and the goals you want to achieve. It's a very simple tool, but it is also effective.

In the first step, write down your current status. Where are you right now? Be truthful. Consider your pain points, and the things you most want out of life. It might be more time with your family. It might be earning more money. Everyone will be different. Write down your truth about where you are right now.

In the next step, write your compelling vision of what you want your life to look like in one year. In the next step, describe why this vision is so important. Your WHY is your driving force. It gets you up and out of bed every morning.

Finally, write down the capabilities and tools that you think are needed to reach those goals.

This can serve as a nice roadmap, a blueprint for your future. Ideally, work with a friend or coach to complete this exercise.

Conclusion

I hope this book has provided you with the guidance and encouragement that you need in order to get past the fears and worries that come with moving to Canada for your education, employment, and life.

There will be tough times ahead. There will be times that you want to quit. However, my experience is proof that it can be done. You too can do the things that you put your mind to as long as you have a plan.

If there's one thing I love to do, it's to teach people how to replicate my success and do it NOW.

How important is it to take action today? I will leave you with the words of author Marc Levy:

> If you want to know the value of one year, just ask a student who failed a course.
>
> If you want to know the value of one month, ask a mother who gave birth to a premature baby.
>
> If you want to know the value of one hour, ask the lovers waiting to meet.

> If you want to know the value of one minute, ask the person who just missed the bus.
>
> If you want to know the value of one second, ask the person who just escaped death in a car accident.
>
> And if you want to know the value of one-hundredth of a second, ask the athlete who won a silver medal in the Olympics.

If you are ready to get started, sign up now for my **Bonus Training**: *How to Start Right Your Study, Work, and Life in Canada.* You can access it at **StartRightBook.com/training.**

"If we are related," said the immortal Emerson, "we shall meet." May I borrow his thought, tweak it just a little, and say, "If we are related, we have met, through these pages."

Remember, you are just one habit away….

A Note to Parents

"Children have to be educated, but they have also to be left to educate themselves."– Ernest Dimnet

To all the parents out there: even though this book is aimed primarily at your children, it is equally important to you. After all, you are the ones with the courage to let your children go to school on the other side of the world because you know it will present them with some wonderful opportunities they would not experience otherwise.

Parents want the best for their children, naturally. They want to make sure their children get a great education and that they have a great life. Parents also know that sometimes the best chance of success for a child is to have them become an international student. It can be a gift that gives a child the best chance to succeed academically, personally, and professionally, all while living globally.

Parents often try to exert a substantial amount of control over their children, though, and often this control continues even after the child is older and capable of making decisions and acting responsibly. It is important for parents to support their children, certainly, but they also need to give their children space and empower those children to experiment, even when it risks failure.

There are good orientation and transition programs that can help your children as they head to their new school. There are often special programs designed for international students, as well as cross-cultural programs that might help. Learn as much as possible about where your child will be going. Help them research the types of items they are going to need when they arrive. Even though they are going to be taking on a lot of responsibility, it does not mean you cannot provide them with some guidance, and, where necessary, financial support. Of course, you still want to let your child learn to stand on their own feet. But that is a process, and it will not happen overnight.

I am the son of two loving parents. They wanted me to be happy and become a Canadian citizen. They wanted me to have opportunities that I would not have had otherwise in Kazakhstan. They always told me that parents should give their children wings to fly and a home to come back to. I think their philosophy is beautiful and I aspire to be that kind of parent to my own child. Prepare your children, support them, and love them, but let them learn, and provide them with space. Be an invisible cushion that is there for them if they need it.

When your child leaves, you will likely experience what is known as the empty nest syndrome. You will experience a lot of different emotions when you let your child go so far away. I know it hurts, but it is often what is best for them. You are brave and you need to stay calm for their sake. If you do not express confidence in them, they may never have the courage to leave home.

Goodbye now does not mean goodbye forever. There will be visits, and technology has made it possible to communicate whenever you want. Talk with your child. Ask them to come up with a communication plan to stay in touch.

You should also keep busy now that your child is gone. Visit your friends more often or start a new hobby or even a business. By keeping busy, keeping in touch, and learning to accept the inevitable, both you and your child will be happier and stronger.

If you would like some help coaching your child, or if you want to know more about the strategies in this book and how ultimately they could help your child succeed in studies, work, and life in Canada, please reach out to us. We are here for your child but, recognizing what an important part you play in that success, we are here for you, too.

Head over to **StartRightBook.com/speak** to apply.

www.ingramcontent.com/pod-product-compliance
Lightning Source LLC
Chambersburg PA
CBHW070043120526
44589CB00035B/2295